Don't Be A D!ck

HR Advice for a Kinder, Healthier,
and More Successful Workplace

By: Lindsay K. Mattes, MAOL

ISBN: 979-8-9897666-3-5
Library of Congress Control Number: 2024908906

Follow Lindsay Mattes
Social Media Outlets:
LinkedIn - Lindsaykmattes
Facebook - Lindsay Simons Mattes
TikTok - hrmama6
Insta - mamamattes
Email: website:https://www.lindsaymattes.com/

Dedication

To my family.

Jack Duffy Mattes – you always have my back and believe that I can do anything, whether it's writing a book, running a ½ marathon, or holding sheetrock above my head. You give me faith that I will accomplish my goals. Thanks for being the hottest, most charming husband at every work party, fundraiser, business conference and dinner with colleagues I ask you to attend. I love you.

Ivie – Thank you for helping me write this book, for the hours of conversations, edits and encouragement. You are my north star and your love puts me on the top of the world.

Emma – You are my ride-or-die, my mini-me. Thank you for being the ambassador and glue for the many branches of your family tree. You keep us all connected and close, especially all your sisters.

Izzy - Thank you for sharing your talents with me, including headshots, social media tips, and personal stylist. Thank you for your honesty, accountability, and for holding the space for me to be better.

Gracie – Thank you for the research, marketing and administrative support you've provided for this book. You are a whirlwind of color, energy, and tenacity that lights up all the people around you and powers our lives.

Ian - You have become an anchor in our family. Your patience, love, and support keep us grounded and make us better. It takes an amazing person to join our brood!

Laura - Thanks for walking down this HR path with me, it's been a wild and wonderful ride, and I couldn't have done it without you. Thanks for choosing to be part of our family.

You all have taught me so much about authenticity and courage. You have supported and pushed me; loved and endured me through not just writing this book, but on our family journey. It wasn't always pretty, but there was always love and I hope, kindness in our home.

Acknowledgments

I've always had this book inside of me, but I didn't know how, when, or if it would ever really happen. Then I went to a friend's book signing; proud to support her and celebrate her accomplishment. That's when I met Dr. Denise Nicholson, and my book journey began. Thanks, Kathy White, for inspiring me and putting me in the right room, with the right person, at the right time.

To the many amazing colleagues, leaders and teammates I have met along the way; you taught me what truly caring for your employees can achieve. You showed me, by example, the value of true respect and conscious culture creation within organizations. I also want to thank the Dicks that I have worked for, and with, throughout my career. I am grateful for the lessons you taught me, good, bad, and indifferent. They all caused me to grow and some even got you included in this book.

A special shoutout to my brother, Sean. Thanks for your willingness to be an example in the book. And thanks for all the times when you weren't the asshole, but the confidant I needed. Don't worry – I won't tell anyone!

Thank you to the smart, hardworking, loving, supporting women I am lucky to have in my life. Kristin Acree, Ellen Paddock, Dany Bjerregaard, Emily Terrell, Laura Hansell, Jennifer Schild, Kristy James, Julia Franklin, Jamie Lawson, Rebecca Yurth, Angie Curtis, Holly Berk, Adrienne Thomas, Marabeth Passannante, Mackenzie Ertmann, Whitney Johnson, Diana Baxter, Tina Hazlett, Elisa Garn, Jo Aldridge, Nikki Johnston, Lindsey Taylor, Kate Gewecke, and so many more! Whether we work together, play together, have been friends forever or we just met. You taught me the value and power of female friendships and solidarity in diversity.

Thank you to my Writer's Incubator class, your feedback, encouragement, support and love gave me the strength to cross the finish line.

Bold Academy classmates, your honest and kind feedback makes me a better speaker, leader and friend.

I want to thank Bold Publishing for partnering with me to get this book to completion, including editing, printing, designing and marketing.

Finally, I want to thank Dr. Denise Nicholson. You took a chance on a white girl from Utah and believed in me. You stuck with me as I stumbled and fumbled my way through this process; holding space for me when I wasn't ready, encouraging me when I was, and pushing me when I needed it most.

This book would not exist without you.

Contents

"Kindness today is an act of rebellion."

- Pink

Introduction

What's in a name?" asks Juliet "A rose by any other name would smell as sweet." The same is true of HR. Whether Human Resources (HR), Personnel or People Operations – it is the heart of your organization, even if you are an organization of one. It is our responsibility to facilitate a workplace of safety, respect, diversity and kindness; in other words, a successful and positive culture. HR is described as the department responsible for walking the fine line between what is best for the organization and advocating for the employees, but I disagree. HR should not be walking a tightrope but rather blazing a trail of authentic relationships and organizational collaboration where every employee is valued, respected, and treated with kindness. We see the best and worst sides of our employees. Through their successes and their struggles, we learn a lot about human behavior. It is our responsibility to share our expertise and experience with our employees because a kinder workplace makes a kinder world. So why is the title of my book don't be a dick . . . divine intervention!

There I was, standing in a state-of-the-art training room, enthusiastically delivering the one-of-a-kind presentation that I had designed to be engaging and funny while still being authentic and powerful. I had skipped the history slides that discussed Title VII of the Civil Rights Act[1] followed by a timeline of amendments and laws intended to make the workplace free from discrimination. There were no video clips from the 1980s as they tend to be out-of-date, irrelevant, and more amusing than helpful in their ridiculousness. My training was not going to focus on the regulations requiring companies to treat employees as humans or the millions of dollars companies have had to pay for disregarding these laws. Don't misunderstand, the regulations are embarrassingly necessary; but I wanted to focus on treating employees fairly because it's the right thing to do, not because you're legally obligated. I was confident this approach would move the managers to a deeper level of understanding.

The first 15 minutes went great. I was keeping it lively, funny and, I thought, interactive. I then presented a real-life scenario to the managers and asked an easy, open-ended question believing it would lead to an honest conversation. I looked around expecting to see hands raised with insightful thoughts and questions. Instead, I was met with a wall of silence. My stomach dropped and imposter syndrome started

---

1. The Civil Rights Act of 1964 is a landmark civil rights and labor law in the United States that outlaws discrimination based on race, color, religion, sex, and national origin.

creeping through my veins as I understood the silence. I wasn't inspiring them; I was boring and/or confusing them. Most of the attendees were typing on their phones, skimming through the written presentation aimlessly or nodding off; I swear at least one guy was just outright sleeping with drool streaming down the left side of his mouth. The few managers who were trying to pay attention were looking at me blankly because they were expecting 15 minutes of the history of equal employment opportunities, starting with the famous black and white photo of Lyndon Johnson handing Martin Luther King Jr. a pen after signing the Civil Rights Act of 1964[2]. At least they were paying close enough attention to recognize something unusual was happening.

I was devastated; then I was pissed. Gone was the imposter syndrome, my veins were pumping with anger. Damn them, this is important! I had worked hard to humanize the impact harassment has on people, so they could understand the importance of respect. Of course, I knew which manager needed which section of the presentation, and as I held the gaze of the one whose behavior had prompted this training in the first place, my mouth overtook my brain and I blurted out, "You know, just don't be a Dick!" I immediately gasped and covered my mouth with my hands. There was a moment

---

2. President Johnson shakes hands with The Rev. Martin Luther King after handing him a pen during the signing of the Civil Rights bill into law during a White House ceremony 7/2. July 2. Photograph. Retrieved from the Library of Congress, www.loc.gov/item/2005681248/.

when the world just stopped, and as I looked out to a room full of suddenly alert employees, they all burst out laughing. The simple statement, in familiar and authentic vernacular, had changed the energy in the room. The engagement with my audience that I had been chasing the entire session appeared. People shifted in their chairs, opened their bodies up, unfolded their arms and sat up a bit straighter. I saw a glimmer of understanding flit through many eyes and even saw a light bulb going on for a few. As the laughter died down, the questions and responses came in:

"What exactly does it mean?"

"What do you do when someone is being a jerk to you?"

"People are just too sensitive these days."

"What if I'm not being a jerk, but someone is taking it personally to get me in trouble?"

As the question-and-answer session continued, the energy in the room got more electric. I wasn't the only one answering questions. The managers were talking *to* each other instead of *at* each other. We were having a true discussion; I could see the potential of that team when they were honestly communicating. It was a magical moment and I felt so proud of myself and my managers, things were going to change.

Except they didn't. While funny, my impromptu declaration didn't magically make everything better, not permanently anyway. In fact, the change we'd discovered together began evaporating as soon as we left the room.

It was immediate for some, the issues they faced after just 1 hour away from their desks dragged them back into real life. Others lasted longer, but the reality of day-to-day life; the deadlines, project delays and people out for themselves, is exhausting. There is also loneliness and disillusionment in trying to change yourself. Especially when it feels like no one else is trying. Even with a catchy phrase, we fall back into our old habits because change is hard and no one can be perfect. I wanted to continue that dialogue. I wanted to bring it out of the training room and into practice; I wanted to write a book.

This book emerged from many years of awkward and ineffective anti-harassment training. It contextualizes excessively restrictive policies that were crafted in response to a single unprecedented incident or someone imagining a "worst-case scenario" which causes inflexibility and frustration in real-world situations. It evolved from navigating petty and childish arguments between co-workers and watching managers trying to be nice instead of kind. (We'll address the difference in Chapter 2.)

It also originated from authentic, honest conversations; from vulnerability and kindness, from those moments in life when you truly connect with another person. It developed from watching relationships change and evolve, experiencing true partnership moments; and celebrating when personal and company goals exceed expectations. It was ready to be written when I understood the message that I wanted to convey; the heart of my mission and vision for HR. The big secret is that we need to be kinder to one another.

The theory of kindness in the workplace is not new, yet it continues to be frequently overlooked. Much like HR, there are many different words used to express the same ideas. It was during my pursuit of a master's degree in organizational leadership that I initially encountered the idea of practicing kindness in the workplace. Gonzaga University offered a certificate program in Servant Leadership, a leadership paradigm introduced by Robert Greenleaf in his 1970 essay, *The Servant as Leader*[3].

Greenleaf's philosophy emphasizes leaders' primary role as servants to their teams or organizations, focusing on their well-being, growth and development. He believed that leaders should prioritize serving and empowering others; helping them reach their potential, rather than solely focusing on their own authority and interests. This approach to leadership has since gained traction and has been incorporated into leadership development and organizational management practices.

The Arbinger Institute[4] refers to this approach as cultivating an "Outward Mindset." The outward mindset

3. Greenleaf, Robert K. "The Servant as Leader." The Robert K. Greenleaf Center for Servant Leadership, 1970, https://www.greenleaf.org/what-is-servant-leadership/.

4. a global leadership development firm that helps organizations shift their mindsets, transform their cultures, and drive changes that lead to exceptional results https://arbinger.com/.

revolves around seeing others as individuals with their own needs, objectives and challenges, rather than focusing solely on oneself. This mindset encourages empathy and understanding, leading to better collaboration, communication and problem-solving. It emphasizes the transformation of one's perspective from self-centeredness to a more inclusive and compassionate outlook.

In 2016, the U.S. Chamber of Commerce Foundation released a business case for kindness, saying "Kindness is critical to the full expression and embodiment of [company] values because they are rooted in the ability of people to interact in positive and constructive ways, with confidence and support."[5] Harvard Business Review said, "When leaders and employees act kindly towards each other, they facilitate a culture of collaboration and innovation."[6]

HR is the place where you can speak plainly and honestly. It is the place you feel the safest . . . right? I believe it is, or should be, and whether you agree or disagree this is the right book for you. I know with simple, straightforward and authentic dialogue we can make HR the safe space it should be and I'm here to walk you through how we can make that happen!

---

5. US Chamber of Commerce Foundation. "The Business Case for Kindness." Business Kindness: The Power of Creating a Compassionate Economy, https://www.uschamberfoundation.org/business-kindness/business-case-kindness.

6. Management Tip of the Day. "Don't Underestimate the Power of Kindness at Work." Harvard Business Review, 18 May 2021, https://hbr.org/2021/05/dont-underestimate-the-power-of-kindness-at-work.

In the following pages, I share my professional journey in HR through stories and examples from "real life"; heartbreaks and successes that continue to light my path toward more kindness at work and in life. Each chapter addresses common workplace scenarios and situations where managers and employees behaved unprofessionally and details potential alternatives to produce a better outcome. I'll also share moments when kindness was successful and improved the teams and companies where it was practiced.

However far you want to take the path, everyone can practice kindness. So, settle in, buckle up and get ready for a funny, poignant look at corporate life from the HR office, showing the dangers of being a Dick and the success practicing kindness can have within your organization and your life.

For me, that includes a lot of humor, often of the self-deprecating kind, a bit of sass (okay maybe more than a bit) and a sincere belief that kindness is what our organizations, families and our world needs. I will make jokes and share controversial ideas, just go with me; after all – it's why you picked up a book with a controversial title.

Oh, and don't worry; the names except my family have been changed and stories have been combined to protect the guilty, the innocent, and to avoid being sued.

"Think before you speak, your words could hurt
someone's feeling more than you intended it to"

~Justin Bieber

Chapter 1
Who is Dick?

"Sticks and stones may break my bones, but words will never hurt me."

What a lie we were told with this fun nursery rhyme. Words matter and they can hurt much more than a broken bone. Words can also heal, protect and provide peace. Often the difference is only in the understanding, or misunderstanding, of the word itself. Words need definition, context and sometimes clarification. When I said, "Don't be a Dick" in that training, it was clear I wasn't talking about a person, but a pattern of behavior. The word can be exchanged for any number of synonyms, the behavior is the same regardless of the name that rings authentic for you. I like to switch it up, depending on the audience. This behavior is exhibited by individuals who show a lack of respect and consideration for others. It involves actions that are dismissive, insensitive and careless of any impact to those around them. It's non-discriminate. It can be conscious or subconscious; intentional or unintentional;

occasional or chronic. It's a universal behavior every one of us has engaged in and will engage in again. We all have those moments, but it's possible to recognize them, learn from them and do better next time.

This behavior falls into three categories: Intentional, Accidental, and Conscientious. The Intentional Dick deliberately, or carelessly, harms another person; either through purposeful actions or calculated behavior. Accidental Dick behavior is caused by being unaware of, or lacking information about, how their actions might be insensitive, disrespectful or harmful. Basically, they don't realize how they are being perceived. Conscientious behavior refers to someone who is practicing kindness. They try to pay attention to their language and actions. They apologize and try again when they make a mistake. We are not perfect. Perfection is a myth, but practice makes us better. So, keep practicing, learning, and extending your ability to be kind.

Intentional

There are two main classes that fall within this category. Some people adopt the behavior as a personality trait, taking pride in being an intentional jerk. So much so that they are willing to fight for their right to be a schmuck, for what behavior they believe is valid or as a personality trait . This is my preferred type of intentional Dick, at least you know where you stand with them. When they say offensive or hurtful words or their actions cross the line, you shouldn't be caught off guard, they warn you.

The other variety is disguised. They know the impact of their words, but play it off as a joke, a misunderstanding, or resort to gaslighting[7]. You know, they're the ones being jerks, but suddenly they act like you're the one causing the problem. Instead of admitting their behavior, they get defensive and angry; basically making it your fault. While neither is a pleasant experience, I prefer transparency to duplicitousness.

My brother Sean is my favorite example of the first group. Sean is a self-proclaimed asshole. He's also the one who reminded me of the importance of self-identification. When I told him that he was my example of an Intentional Dick, he immediately corrected me and said, "asshole". He wasn't the least bit concerned about being in the book, he just wanted to be described in his preferred vernacular; the word he uses to describe his identity. Adjusting my language to respect him is one of the easiest ways to practice kindness.

One Saturday afternoon, while hanging out at my mom's house with some of my siblings, I brought up the topic of workplace safety. At the time, my role had expanded to Interim Safety Manager, possibly the only vital department more dismissed than HR, and I was sharing some of my challenges with enforcing new policies. Not thrilling dialogue,

7. Gaslighting is a manipulative tactic in which someone deliberately distorts or denies facts, events, or reality to make another person doubt their own perceptions, memories, or sanity.

but it seemed like an innocuous topic; something we try to do for Mom, she hates it when we fight.

I mentioned I was getting pushback about securing the external doors and requiring the employees to wear their badges in a visible location. No more keeping it in your pocket so you can beep the door open with your butt. There were multiple reasons we had decided to tighten up security. I had recently run into a stranger wandering alone through the building. This was a manufacturing plant with easily transportable and valuable supplies; including raw materials, like sheets of aluminum, finished products boxed and ready to be shipped and office equipment with confidential, proprietary and classified information stored in them. We had also recently done a round of layoffs and not everyone knew the employees who had been impacted. Finally, there had been several workplace shootings in the news in the prior month and it was at the forefront of the workplace safety officers' minds. As I was expressing my frustration and confusion about the employee's response, Sean jumped in with his perspective.

"That is such a ridiculous rule. As if a 'BADGE,'" he says with air quotes and disdain, "will protect anyone from being shot." Did I mention my brother is a history teacher in a Junior High School, one of the places most frequently targeted in the current run of mass shootings? I was momentarily surprised, but Sean likes to say contrary things, just for the sake of being contrary. I chuckled and responded, "Of course, the badge isn't going to protect you from a gun, but it provides another level of security. At least you know whether someone is supposed to be in the building."

He laughed, shrugged his shoulders, and replied, "I've worked there for 15 years, everyone knows who I am. I don't need a badge to prove I should be there."

I quipped back in a slightly sharper tone, "As the person who is responsible for terminations, I can say with certainty that we don't make an announcement to the entire company when someone has been let go. It's generally frowned upon."

"Whatever", he says nonchalantly, "I won't be forced to follow stupid policies. I just laugh every time Keith comes by and tells me to wear my badge." He then proudly admits, "I just tell him, 'Hey you know me, I'm not going to ever wear this badge. I'm an asshole.'" Followed by a shrug, silently saying: *What're they going to do?*

To be clear, your Health, Environmental and Safety Team is aware that requiring employees to wear visible photo badges is, most likely, not a deterrent for someone trying to cause harm in your building. However, it is an efficient way for first responders and police to determine victims from perpetrators. Less dramatically, it is someone's job to enforce the rule; your colleague and work friend. They may laugh with you and agree it's a silly rule, but inside they are begging you to just wear the effing badge. They are getting heat from their boss because you aren't following the rules.

If giving your colleagues a little leeway isn't enough motivation to adhere to the policy, consider the impact on your reputation and the regard in which you are held within the organization. It might seem like your actions go unnoticed, but there's always someone observing and learning from you – whether that influence is positive or negative. This holds particularly true for younger individuals. While teenagers might not openly "respect" teachers, many are looking up to them for guidance. Take Sean, for instance. He might have an anti-establishment stance, yet he's viewed as an authority figure. Not only are students watching, but so are parents and fellow educators. Even Keith, the security guard, is taking cues from his behavior. By refusing to wear a badge, you're sending a message that abiding by rules is unnecessary and breaking them is admirable or cool. On the other hand, wearing the badge sends a message of unity and respect.

The management team, those of us who write the rules, are also watching and receiving updates. Guaranteed that a buddy of yours who says, "It's cool, just between you and me", is spilling their guts when it's their job on the line. They are absolutely going to confirm you are the issue and your employment status will be impacted by the dissent. Behaving in that way will negatively impact your job status, perhaps not immediately, but eventually.

After his declaration, the room got quiet. I made eye contact with another sibling and could see we were having a similar thought. However, Dave is the diplomat and peacemaker in the family and goes out of his way to de-escalate potential family drama, so when he slightly shook his head, I knew he wasn't going to wade in. Normally, I am NOT the diplomat. In fact, I pride myself on being the outspoken, rebellious, black sheep/heathen in my otherwise very religious family. I rarely shy away from the opportunity to share a differing perspective. . . or pick a fight, depending on my mood. Sean isn't the only one who can be an intentional troublemaker, I also have my moments. Dave didn't have to worry that day because I was too flabbergasted to get on my soapbox. It was almost verbatim what an employee had told me that day. I looked at Sean, shook my head, and disappointingly said, "You really are a Dick," to which he responded, "Asshole, I'm an asshole."

Accidental

The behavior of an Accidental Dick is transitional. It is the crossroads between Intentional and Conscientious behavior, and it exposes the underlying motivations based on your secondary actions. Once you realize, whether through personal reflection or external feedback, that you've hurt or offended someone you are faced with the opportunity to choose.

Distinguishing between unintentional and intentional behavior can be challenging, both to the observer and the actor. There are times when people are just oblivious. Whether they are willfully ignorant or just not paying attention, an accidental jerk doesn't walk into a situation determined to cause harm or offense. Regardless of their intent, the result remains the same, their behavior caused a negative impact on someone.

During a software implementation project where there had been several issues causing a less than smooth or pleasant transition, one of the vendors sent an email requesting a change in the format of a meeting. The meeting was planned to be in person, but that morning they sent an email requesting to move the meeting to virtual. The end of the message confirmed that if a virtual meeting was not possible they could still come into the office. The intent of the email was clear, there had been a change of plans and virtual was going to work better than in person.

Before anyone else could answer, a team member promptly hit "reply all" and said, "I am prepared to have an in-person meeting today." That was it. The question wasn't even directly answered. First, it didn't address the actual question of Zoom or Teams, nor did it say, "I would prefer to have the meeting in person, if possible", followed by answering the actual question. Nope, just a rather nonsensical response to ALL. Gotta love reply all – it can be a powerful and dangerous tool. I'm confident at least 80% of all HR professionals can tell you a cringe-worthy "reply all" story. Those stories are better suited for my future podcast, *HR After Hours*.

The rest of the team promptly responded to the original email, expressing their willingness to conduct the meeting virtually and confirming that Zoom was their preferred platform. They assured the vendor that there was no need for them to come to the office. Within 30 minutes, Brad, the one who had replied all, visited the HR office to inform us about the change to a virtual meeting, in case we had missed his email. We all confirmed that we had indeed read the emails and were comfortable with the virtual format. Brad then went on to explain the entire email exchange, inadvertently coming across as condescending, and concluded with the statement, "Given the choice, I will always choose an in-person meeting."

When he finally left the HR office I turned to my colleague and said, "Do you think he knows he's being a Dick?" Despite the flippant way I asked the question, she paused to really consider the question. Her answer surprised me, "I don't think so. I think it's accidental." But I wasn't sure; so I tried to recall all of my previous interactions with Brad.

In determining Accidental versus Intentional it's important to pay attention to context clues. What do we know about Brad as a person? What prior experiences have we had with him, particularly in similar situations? Equally significant is observing how he reacts when he realizes he has inadvertently caused offense.

Most of us are simply trying to live our lives. We go to work and do our jobs and then go home and enjoy our hobbies. Our intentions typically do not revolve around causing disruption or harm to others. How we respond when we discover we've hurt someone is the crossroads. This is the point where we face a choice; accidental either becomes intentional or conscientious. Do we choose to dig in and staunchly defend ourselves, justifying our behavior? Feeling defensive and attempting to explain yourself is a natural response, especially when you are unaware that your words or actions could be offensive. It's common to believe that your intent should take precedence over the impact of your words or actions, but that's not true. You do not have to like someone, believe what they are saying, or agree with them, but you don't get to decide how they feel.

Or do you opt for a different path, taking a deep breath and setting aside your immediate feelings of hurt or anger? Instead, making a conscious effort to listen to the other person's perspective; stepping back and resisting the urge to act impulsively in response to an unexpected reaction. This is being Conscientious; it's practicing kindness.

Conscientious

Being conscientious means practicing Maya Angelou's advice, "Do the best you can until you know better. Then when you know better, do better." It's important to remember that all of us can and will be jerks sometimes, it's not just an occasional occurrence and can be a daily challenge. The key is when finding yourself with the choice, try to make the decision to be kind.

Being conscientious does not entail tiptoeing around and avoiding anything that might be considered "offensive." It's not about adhering to a rigid sense of "political correctness," if that term even holds meaning anymore. True conscientiousness centers on the values of learning, personal growth and embracing our shared humanity. It is about seeing the person in front of you and offering them kindness.

Kindness can manifest in various ways: through respect, trust, or simply giving the benefit of the doubt. As Steven R. Covey states, "Most people do not listen to understand; they listen to respond." Practicing kindness involves actively listening to the information, taking time to contemplate it, and showing openness to recognizing and acknowledging someone else's perspective. This principle applies to both those who feel offended and those who may have unintentionally caused offense.

Many years ago, I had a colleague named Matthew. We didn't work in the same department, but our jobs overlapped, and we would be in occasional meetings together. He always went by Matthew in our meetings, so I didn't even think about it, until I called him Matt. Here's a secret about me . . . I love nicknames and have a slight compulsion to shorten people's names, regardless of the length. My oldest daughters have 4 letter names on purpose, Ivie and Emma. The assumption being I wouldn't need to shorten it. I call them Iv & Em.

Back to Matthew. One summer we both joined the company volleyball team and got to know each other better. As I felt more comfortable with him the natural thing for me was to start calling him Matt. Matthew is such a formal name and now that we were on the same company volleyball team, we were friends and friends have nicknames for each other. At practice that day, I called him Matt. When I did, he stiffened just a bit, his eyes hardened slightly and the energy coming from him changed. He politely said, "It's Matthew". I was taken aback and immediately thought, "Well that's dumb, Matthew is so formal and takes a long time to say. It's a compliment when I give someone a nickname. Why is he so stuck-up?" These were only some of the things that ran through my head when he corrected me. It was that knee-jerk reaction you get when you suddenly realize you've said or done something "wrong", and you feel uncomfortable and embarrassed. Additionally, sarcasm is my first language (see Sean's story).

Before I responded, the kinder, less sarcastic side kicked in and I thought, "What difference does it make? It's his name, if he wants to be called Matthew, just call him Matthew. Hell, do you really care if he wants to be called Sir Matthew? Probably, you won't continue to hang around him, if he goes with Sir Matthew, but Matthew is easy." I nodded slightly and repeated back, "Matthew", acknowledging it made a difference to him and reassured him that I would respect it. The most amazing thing happened then; he released a breath I hadn't even realized he was holding. His eyes softened again and he smiled back. I realized he had been expecting pushback like my initial thoughts. This may have been my first time with the experience, but it wasn't his. This was something that had clearly caused him to be teased, mocked, or even dismissed more than once.

From then on, I made a conscious effort to call him Matthew. In the beginning, it wasn't easy; it went against my nature. Nicknames are one of my love languages, whether people, pets, or inanimate objects. I would slip and say Matt, but I would immediately apologize and correct myself and before long, it was just his name; it wasn't hard. And to this day, I remember him as Matthew.

Pronouns are the same thing. We all have pronouns like we all have names, and the only person's pronouns you should care about are your own. Why would you care about anyone else's? It has zero impact on your life but may mean a great deal to the individual you're speaking with. You don't have to understand or agree with their pronouns; it is irrelevant whether they make sense to you. It might make you uncomfortable and feel hard to adjust to, but when you practice, you get better. When you know something is important to another person, regardless of your feelings about it, when you are Conscientious you address them in the way they have asked to be addressed.

I was working with an organization facing this issue during a growth period. The organization was well-known in the community and relied heavily on its reputation for funding and community support. They were very successful and ready to grow the organization and expand their services to a wider demographic. One of the main goals was updating their brand; it was time to revitalize. The building was getting a fresh coat of paint, the logo was modernized, and the letterhead was updated. One of the final changes was to update the company email signature. You want everyone to have a consistent signature line, just as much as you want everyone to use the same letterhead.

When it comes to email signatures, the easiest way to ensure consistency is to have a template for all employees. When they set up their email, they add their information to the template and that's it. Everyone matches for a while, but then they can't find the template, so you copy and paste from someone else, and so on, and so on until you have 5-10 different signatures, all like each other, but not quite the same. This is where they were, so when the new template was rolled out, it was expected; but it was also surprising to some of the staff. The community was growing and becoming more diverse, this meant the applicant pool was also becoming more diverse. HR had their pronouns included in their signature lines as did most of the newer employees. It's a simple message to employees and applicants that an organization practices diversity, equity and inclusion. The new template did not include space for pronouns. The leadership team had decided not to include space for pronouns, as they didn't believe it represented the best image in their relatively conservative community and organizational culture.

The HR team disagreed and brought their concerns to the leadership team to open a dialogue. There were a variety of opinions to navigate. Some people were 100% against them and some wholeheartedly agreed with the addition and thought they should be mandatory. Both sides were concerned not only about the optics of the situation, but they also felt it was a moral issue. The majority (surprise, surprise) fell in the middle. While they didn't necessarily understand it, they wanted to be inclusive for their staff and families. As the team discussed the situation, people expressed their views and asked questions. There were contentious moments, but the team was committed to working together. After several discussions, they arrived at a compromise. The template included space for pronouns if employees wanted to include them, but they weren't listed on the template. No one declared their grasp of a new concept and accepted it with open arms, mostly because this is a real-life situation, not a contrived one. However, they opted to practice kindness and leave room for personal choice, which actually aligned much more closely with the company's brand and culture than a hardline one way or the other did.

"Niceness tends to border on people-pleasing and can be disingenuous, while kindness is honest yet sensitive to other people's experiences."

~Andrew Swinand

Chapter 2
Nice and Kind Are Not the Same

In the realm of interpersonal behavior, it's essential to recognize the nuanced relationship between being kind and being nice. Kindness encompasses a depth of genuine compassion and benevolence, extending beyond mere social conventions. Acts of kindness often involve a sincere desire to contribute positively to others' well-being, demonstrating empathy, and engaging in considerate gestures that may not necessarily align with conventional niceties. Kindness is rooted in a profound understanding of the Human Experience, and its impact tends to be more profound and lasting than the surface-level politeness associated with being nice.

On the other hand, niceness primarily revolves around agreeable and socially acceptable behavior. While being nice can create a positive and pleasant atmosphere in social interactions, it doesn't always embody the same depth of empathy or intentional goodwill found in acts of kindness. Niceness can sometimes be a superficial adherence to societal norms, characterized by politeness and friendliness without necessarily reflecting a genuine concern for others' well-being. The distinction lies in the motivation behind the behavior – kindness emanates from a place of authentic care, while niceness can occasionally border on being a transactional and socially expected response.

In essence, while kind actions can often be perceived as nice, niceness doesn't consistently convey the same level of genuine kindness. Recognizing this distinction allows us to appreciate the profound impact of intentional acts of kindness that go beyond surface-level pleasantries, fostering meaningful connections and enriching the fabric of human interactions.

Now, let's chat about performance reviews for a minute. You know, those annual meetings that are supposed to be the heart-to-heart talks between manager and employee? The ones meant to set goals, give feedback and create a space where everyone can share their wins and woes? Yeah, those. Ideally, that's the whole purpose behind them – a chance for open communication and understanding between employees and their managers. But let's be real for a second – how many of us have actually felt that warm and fuzzy side of performance reviews?

Have you ever had a performance review that felt more like a genuine heart-to-heart and less like a scripted exchange of niceties? Who has gone into a performance review and come out feeling loved, supported, and clear about your goals? Did you transparently and honestly discuss your strengths and your challenges, your successes and your trials? Have you had the opportunity to discuss what you learned from both the losses and the wins? Probably not.

Performance reviews are dreaded, often delayed, and rarely are a true representation of the employee or the manager. They are usually seen as a chore for the managers; and for employees, a hope filled trip to the principal's office to pick up their report card, ideally to get paid for A's.

While the idea and intention of performance reviews is honorable, the system is flawed. Instead of enhancing communication and increasing collaboration, it's an annual checklist to justify salary increases and an effective tool for increasing anxiety and lowering employee morale. In fact, neuroscientists are discovering that the mere idea of a ranked performance review "provokes a 'fight or flight' response, which gets in the way of 'thoughtful, reflective conversations.'" [8]

Providing effective feedback is a skill, especially if the feedback is intended to be constructive. "Soft skills", better known as leadership skills, rarely take precedence or priority within most companies. Especially when they are looking to lower their bottom line and increase their profits. If a new manager is lucky, HR or their manager will recommend the book *2600 Phrases for Effective Performance Reviews* by Paul Falcone so they have a place to start; albeit an outdated one.

---

8. Gavett, Gretchen. "Why Your Brain Hates Performance Reviews." strategy+business. https://hbr.org/2014/09/why-your-brain-hates-performance-reviews.

Often, they are just given the forms to complete, provided the approved merit increase, and told to get them all done within a month.

As much as employees hate performance reviews, managers hate them more. They don't want to give a bad review any more than the employee wants to receive it, so they try to be nice. Nice can come from a place of kindness; nice can equal kind. Nice can also come from a place of comfort, or more accurately, discomfort.

An Intentional Dick may take the opportunity to provide feedback that focuses entirely on all the "areas of improvement" as well as every issue they've had with the employee over the previous year. They use it as a battering ram under the guise of helping the employee improve. They then support their niceness by giving the employee the standard 3% increase. Essentially just using the opportunity to vent at an employee and then reward them for sitting through it. Luckily, this isn't a common occurrence. Managers don't want to provide negative feedback, so they are more likely to diminish the performance review process or find a reason to dismiss it altogether, rather than using it to bully employees. The avoidance method allows the manager to appease the employee with the 3% increase, while pushing off the negative conversation, until they get fed up and fire the employee.

Many managers aren't opposed to performance reviews and want to have meaningful conversations with their employees. They want to use the annual review to touch base with their employees; to engage in meaningful dialogue with their team and to strengthen the relationship. They also want to see their team get the increase they have earned and deserve. The preparation process takes time and attention; something in high demand and hard to find even for daily responsibilities. With the best of intentions, they focus on positive, high-scoring reviews. Positive feedback is easier to provide, more encouraging for employees and allows the manager to recommend the full available increase. A nice review is easy to give and leaves everyone with warm fuzzies, accentuating the positive and minimizing the negative.

I am not saying to focus on the negative, but disregarding or misleading the employee on how they are performing to be nice, isn't kind. If the employee is doing well, focusing on successes is a great way to start and end the conversation; using the middle to discuss growth opportunities and goals the employee can set for the upcoming year. Kindness means transparency and courage to discuss the good and the bad; empowering the employees with the knowledge and tools to continue to be successful.

Focusing on the positive and not addressing an employee's true performance, especially if there are big issues impacting their job, isn't kind. If you have an employee struggling to meet expectations, who is told during their review that they are meeting expectations, they will not appreciate the niceties when they find out it isn't true. It is the opposite of kind when that employee finds themselves in the HR office, 10 days, 30 days, or even 10 weeks later, holding their final check because they truly WEREN'T meeting expectations. The desire to spare the employee may feel like it's coming from niceness, but it's a Dick move. Telling an employee they are doing fine when they aren't might be nice for the manager by glossing over a difficult conversation, but isn't kind to the employee who needed the honest feedback and the opportunity to improve. Pretending to be nice because you feel uncomfortable does not equate to practicing kindness.

One executive I worked with subscribed to an employee responsibility approach. This entailed managers providing self-reviews to them with clear evidence of wins and explanations for failures. All their direct reports were managers, so the expectation was each of them should already be aware of how they were performing and were just turning in a report. The intent was sincere, but the outcome often wasn't. This organization utilized the focal point performance review; meaning, all employee performance reviews are done once a year at the same time. I do not recommend this type of performance review system; managers are being asked to take a month out of their lives to provide reviews for anywhere between 1-10+ direct reports while awaiting their own performance review, all due in the same month. And then of course, HR must process all the salary increases, usually turned in on the last day of the month for an effective date of the 1st of that month, requiring retroactive pay, usually calculated and added to the employee check manually. It's a mess for everyone.

This executive, Pat, was all about personal reflection and self-reviewing. Once annual review time came around, they would send out the form to all their direct reports with the expectation that they would complete their portion of the review and return it within 2 weeks. Then Pat would review the employees' work and respond with notes. This exchange happened as many times as was needed until Pat felt the review was completed. Pat would then schedule the review and meet with the employee to have a deeper, more meaningful, discussion. One year, Pat was ahead of the game, a full 3 months ahead of the game Pat approached one of their managers, Jessie, and said, "I'd like you to go ahead and submit your review to me before the holidays. I know it's going to be an easy conversation and that will free you up to focus on your own direct reports in the new year."

Jessie was excited about the prospect and felt she and Pat were on the same page. They had worked together closely on a successful project and believed the experience had deepened and strengthened their relationship. Jessie worked on the review after work hours, reading and rereading it multiple times; making small adjustments that she felt better communicated her skills, accomplishments, and goals for the upcoming year. When she submitted her self-review, just 1 week later, she was confident it would be well received. She sent it electronically as well as slipping a physical copy under Pat's door, knowing Pat preferred to review printed documents. Feeling excited and a bit anxious, she waited for the feedback, and she waited, and she waited.

At first, she thought the delay was because they were so in sync, that Pat didn't even have any feedback to give her, and just forgot to schedule the meeting. As she continued to wait, she made excuses for the delay, reminding herself it was the end of the year, and she knew Pat was preparing a report for the board. At their next one-on-one, Jessie asked when she could expect feedback on her review. Pat quickly responded, "I haven't had a chance to review it, the season was busier than expected. I will get it to you before the end of the year though." Jessie accepted this answer and went back to work.

When the new year arrived, she brought it up again, not mentioning that it had been promised in December. Pat's response was less straightforward this time, "Oh, I just have a couple of things I want to rethink, but I'll get it to you soon." *They're still thinking,* the employee thought. *It's fine, after all, the feedback is almost ready, and the new year has its challenges and deadlines.* At this point, they were still working closely together, even exchanging gifts at Christmas. She did feel a tinge of concern, a niggling feeling at the back of her mind; the type of feeling that flashes by so quickly you aren't even sure it was there. She brushed it off telling herself she was being ridiculous.

When month 3 rolled around without having received any information, except break room conversations about colleague's reviews, she admitted to herself that something had gone terribly wrong. Now she was walking around with a pit in her stomach wondering when the meeting was going to happen. After another couple of weeks, she couldn't stand it anymore and decided to confront the situation and get it over with in her next one-on-one. When she walked into the office, she felt sick. She was walking in blind. She couldn't figure out what the problem might be and worst of all, how bad it might be? After all, Pat had been avoiding her for months. She took a deep breath, walked into the office, and sat across from Pat. The round table in the office was supposed to give her a sense of equality, the confidence to know she was as important as everyone else, but it wasn't working at that moment. Jessie didn't even wait for pleasantries, she just looked Pat in the eyes and said, "I want to discuss my performance review." The room felt electric for a moment, she could feel Pat vacillating between indignance and resolve; resolve won. Pat folded their fingers, setting their chin on top and put on a concerned and sad-parent face. After a deep sigh, they finally said, "I was really shocked by your self-review. I thought we were both on the same page, but it appears we're not quite seeing things the same way." Then they sit back into the chair and say, "I've thought about this a lot, and I've decided I'm not going to give you the review back yet, I want to understand how you could give yourself this score before I finalize my remarks." Pat proceeded to explain to Jessie, for over an hour, how she had only been mediocre throughout the year, and they were quite disappointed when she made a mistake that they believed reflected badly on them. At the very end of this non-discussion, Pat says, "I didn't give this to you before the holidays because I wanted you to have a good season. And I have seen some improvements since then, so I've decided to throw you a bone, and give you a 2% increase instead of 1.5%." Jessie walked out of that room, devastated at not even being given an opportunity to respond. She never did get a copy of the review, but it was submitted to HR for her file without her signature, and she left the company within 3 months of the review.

Pat started with the best of intentions, in fact, in their mind it was a nice gesture to complete the review early. Pat believed Jessie's review would be average, knowing she would be disappointed a little at the 1.5% increase, but recognizing how much that missed deadline had cost Pat. She would then have the holidays to think about and formulate a plan to step up her performance in the new year. Then Pat received Jessie's self-review and things changed. They were not on the same page. Rather than making notes on the review and returning it to Jessie for additional review, Pat went with avoidance. This was Pat's first move away from authentic feedback to hiding behind niceness. They decided it was *nice* to wait until after the holidays, it was *nice* to wait to provide negative feedback and it was *nice* that Pat went ahead and gave her a raise, a bigger raise than Pat believed she deserved. But Pat was just avoiding having an honest conversation with Jessie. They were surprised and uncomfortable with the complete disconnect between them. Pat was pretending to be nice but did not behave kindly at all. Pat wasn't interested in how the situation was impacting Jessie, only that they had to deal with her. The final comment, "throwing you a bone", probably still believing they were being nice, was proof that Pat didn't care about kindness, but only about the convenience of nice.

At the risk of sounding like every grandpa on the planet, if I had a nickel for every time I found myself facing a "for cause" termination while still processing the employee's retroactive pay raise, I'd be a millionaire. Okay, that is a bit of a stretch; but it's more common than you would think. Inevitably, when the manager comes to me with the many reasons the employee (who has recently been told they are meeting expectations) needs to be terminated, and I question the discrepancy between this information and their performance review, the answer is always some version of, "I wanted to be nice." Unfortunately, being nice did not equate to kindness. Kindness means providing meaningful feedback and coaching, and while performance reviews are flawed, they provide a template for communication. Some templates work better than others, and it's important to consider the specific needs of your organization.

"It takes courage to be kind."

— Maya Angelou

Chapter 3
Kindness Takes Courage

If you ask an HR professional what the most important piece of advice for managers is, the answer will be, DOCUMENT, DOCUMENT, DOCUMENT! I'm not kidding, HR professionals don't just say document once, because no one hears it, so it will be repeated at least three times. The minimum number is three, but the actual number directly coincides with the number and frequency of times they have needed to have THIS conversation with the manager. Meaning, that the more often we need to ask, "Have you documented this?" the more times the word document will be repeated.

This is something whispered in ears and screamed from rooftops. PLEASE document what happened! The reality of the business world is if it isn't documented it didn't happen. Of course, just because you didn't write or record an event, that doesn't cause the event to evaporate, but it is much more difficult to determine what happened, especially for those who weren't there at the time of the event.

The imploring tone you hear from your HR team when concerns or recognitions are brought to their attention is not a dramatization or an over-exaggeration, it's a genuine plea for everyone to take note. This advice isn't limited to managers alone; it's applicable to every member of the workforce. Documenting your experiences is not just a mundane task; it is a crucial practice because your observations and insights matter.

Keeping detailed records of your professional encounters can serve various purposes. Firstly, it provides a comprehensive account of your experiences, making it easier to recall specific details and events. This, in turn, empowers you to communicate effectively about your work environment, be it to express concerns or highlight achievements.

Moreover, documenting your experiences is a form of self-advocacy. It allows you to articulate your contributions, challenges faced and milestones achieved. Having a record of your accomplishments is a valuable asset during performance evaluations, promotion conversations, or discussions about career progression.

In the 90's, documentation meant typing it up, printing it off on the dot matrix printer with the 3-page carbon copy paper. Pink went to the employee, Goldenrod to the manager, and the original was saved in the HR file; it meant a long afternoon of paperwork. But today, you can literally speak the words, "Siri – take notes" and then talk out loud to yourself while your phone records everything you say. You don't even have to transcribe the notes, just upload them to the applicable file, and poof, a verbatim transcript of your words. It's so easy, yet very few people do it!

Nonexistent or insufficient documentation is the biggest issue facing HR departments, managers and employees because no one is doing it! Intentional Dicks don't even bother to pretend they document their experiences, assuming their word would be sufficient. It's not. This is the manager who comes to my office and says someone needs to be written up because they aren't meeting their goals. My response is always,

"Have you told them they aren't meeting expectations?" The answers vary depending on their level of practice.

I've had more than one manager respond, "They KNOW what their metrics are, and they KNOW they aren't meeting them."

"Okay, but have you talked to them about it?"

"That's why I'm here, they aren't going to work out, so I'm here to write them up so I can fire them."

There's a high probability the manager looking to create documentation to justify termination, is the same manager that turned in the "Meeting Expectations" review the previous week for this same employee.

Another popular answer is:

"Yes, I have talked to them about it."

"Awesome, what did you say?"

"I told them it was time to step up, I was very clear, and they said they understood. Now they are still doing the same thing." A manager practicing kindness might respond:

"We talked about it in our last one-on-one" or "I mentioned during our last meeting that everyone needed to pay closer attention to issue X."

"Okay, did you take notes of the discussion(s)?"

"Well, it was more of a verbal warning." Or "I shared it during our team meeting, so I guess I could send you an email about it." Side note: Verbal warnings still must be written down; you just don't have to send the notes to the HR team… yet. A good leader usually has some level of documentation, such as an email exchange or a meeting confirmation. They will have at least tried to provide documentation up front.

Whichever way they answer that question, my next question is always, "Did you document it?" and I always receive some version of "Yes, of course" or "Just finishing up." By the way, to all of you who say, "Of course, I documented it" and then proceed to create the information after the fact, we know. We can tell if the information is fresh or remembered. We can also tell if you had a conversation with your employee or if you just recounted the experience on paper when we requested it. Even if you are creating the documentation from memory, doesn't mean you shouldn't document it, but it does impact the authenticity of the documentation because the further away from the event, the less accurate a person's memory becomes. Just be upfront in the notes. It doesn't have to be a big deal just, "Notes created on this date, based on recollections of the conversation between X & Y on this date."

The thing is – documentation is a GOOD thing. If you are worried about documenting a situation or an event, ask yourself, why? Are you trying to be nice to someone and spare them the humiliation of errors or are you nervous about documenting yourself? Documentation, by nature, is a subjective recap of an event. The idea that the information can be objective is a lie corporate America and "mainstream" academia have been selling for many years. You are a person, you do not, nor have you ever lived in a vacuum, you have bias. One of the first lessons I learned in my Intro to Women's Studies class, is to acknowledge and name your bias.

Bias is not inherently negative; it's a fundamental aspect of human decision-making. Without biases, it would be difficult to prioritize or act upon anything, as they serve as lenses through which we interpret the world. Our life experiences and surroundings shape these biases, forming a unique perspective for each individual. The key lies in recognizing and understanding our biases. When done effectively, this awareness can lead to remarkable outcomes. However, biases can also be wielded maliciously, perpetuating harm and inequality.

By acknowledging and actively addressing our biases, we can harness their potential for positive change. This requires ongoing self-reflection, a willingness to consider diverse perspectives, and a commitment to fairness and equity. Ultimately, managing bias is crucial for fostering a more inclusive and just society.

In Chapter 1, I mentioned that people can change to be Intentional or Conscientious and the decision is reflected in the behavior. I was working with a team that was struggling with communication in various areas of the department and the entire team was getting frazzled. The leaders were running around putting out fires and covering under-staffing in various areas; everyone was on a short fuse. There was one employee in particular who the Director was struggling with and was ready to terminate. The manager had gathered the documentation, including the signed performance improvement plan (PIP) document from their most recent discussion. They decided to put this manager on the final warning process: 30 days to shape up or ship out. The manager reached out to the employee to schedule a meeting with the impacted parties, including HR. The first meeting request was innocuous, just requesting a check-in. The employee responded with a request to hold the meeting virtually. The manager responded that they would prefer to have it in person as there would be a few more people in attendance; still trying to be ambiguous about the intent of the meeting while emphasizing its importance.

At this point, the employee realized the "whole gang" was going to be present and the conversation wasn't going to be pleasant.

Reasonably, the employee wanted additional information. She responded with, "I would like to have some information on the purpose of this meeting, I am better able to absorb and respond when I have time to process". In normal circumstances, HR would not recommend putting too much in writing without having the conversation first. Context and tone are difficult to convey in written form. However, the manager didn't stop to ask and frustrated with the multiple issues they were dealing with essentially threw up their hands and said, "Fine, here you go." They then proceeded to outline the concerns, issues and potential next steps that would be discussed at the meeting. When I saw the email on a Friday afternoon I cringed, assuming the conversation was going to be more difficult because if it. On the following Sunday I saw the employee reply come through, but I was so sure it wouldn't be good, that I practiced a boundary and waited until Monday morning to open the email.

Here's the thing – it was amazing! The original email was professional and specific without being too harsh and the response was the same. In fact, the first thing the employee said was to thank the manager for taking the time to write everything out. She then proceeded to detail her response.

The employee acknowledged some areas where she could be doing better, but also discovered that one of the main issues was due to a misunderstanding of responsibilities; course correction was easily addressed when the need was communicated clearly. By the time the meeting took place, it was an open, friendly and productive meeting, with everyone looking for solutions and suggestions to work together better. The manager's email could have tipped the scales. She was frustrated and tired of dancing around the issue so, she decided to do something that could have potentially been perceived as a Dick move.

Remember, an accidental situation is a crossroads with the participants making the choices. There was hope it wouldn't make things worse, but the odds were not in her favor. The manager chose to be conscientious; she accepted the employee's request for additional information and provided it in a professional tone; even including things that had improved. This was exactly what the employee had been looking for. A clear, written understanding of her job responsibilities and the opportunity to process the information and respond professionally.

Documentation is often considered another nice, not kind, trap; an opportunity to fire an employee, or an employee looking to report or even sue the organization. This is a reasonable assumption because that's how it is being used by a large majority of companies and people, but clearly that doesn't have to be the case. The documentation in this case allowed for a true opportunity to make a successful course correction felt by all stakeholders.

"It's me, hi, I'm the problem, it's me."

— Taylor Swift

Chapter 4
Sometimes You're the Dick

We've all met that person who endlessly tells you all the ways people, systems and life in general cause their bad behavior. They are completely innocent of the situations they find themselves in, and everyone else is the problem. And every time I meet them again, I want to say, "What if it's not them, what if it's you?". The truth is, there is some part of almost every Dick-like interaction that you will need to take at least some responsibility for. My mom used to say, "It takes two to have a fight." We may not like to hear it, but that's true.

On my first day at a new company, I had the opportunity to experience that misplaced blame, up close and personal. There I was, in my office, getting settled. I'd gotten a tour of the building, met several of the managers and was scheduled to have lunch with the president and several other members of the Senior Management Team. Mostly, I was just taking a deep breath and trying to take it all in when an employee comes into my office and says, "My check didn't get deposited". Apparently, that was the standard time every employee checked their bank accounts because suddenly multiple people were standing outside my office with the same concern before I could even process the first statement. It seemed no one got paid that day, which was especially bad since it was in fact payday.

It must've been an operator error somewhere in the process, either with the company or with the payroll system. With the deluge of confirmations, the payroll team investigated the situation, and it was discovered the button that needed to be pushed to submit payroll – was forgotten. Oops. Upon recognizing the error, it was immediately submitted, but it can take up to 24 hours to post. Despite not being responsible for payroll, or even employed by the company when the error occurred, the responsibility fell to me to notify all the employees. I sent out an email explaining there had been a delay in processing and that they would receive their payment within 24 hours. I also confirmed that the organization would cover any Overdraft or related fees caused by delay in the deposit. The email included instructions on how to contact their banks, explain the situation and request any fees be reversed. It also included instructions on how to submit any fees that weren't reversed to HR for reimbursement.

Intentional

The issue came up at lunch and it was my first glimpse into the culture and attitude of the management team. As the finance manager was explaining the situation, the president was getting more and more frustrated, asking questions about how it had happened and what the new process would be to ensure it didn't happen again. I was impressed by how it was being handled and chimed in, "Don't worry, we've notified employees and provided guidance on how to get reimbursed for any fees incurred due to our error." The president turned to look at me and said, "Why would we do that?" which was immediately echoed by the finance manager, "That's what I said, but Lindsay says we have to." All eyes turned to me while I was looking around the table baffled. Here's the thing, it isn't easy to render me speechless, I'm more the speak-out-loud until you figure things out and then share out loud the resolution you've discovered, *kinda person*.

While I sat there a bit dumbfounded, the finance manager and president proceeded to explain why the company should not be held responsible for other people's financial difficulties. They were blaming the employees with bounced checks for not being better prepared. When I finally found my voice I said, astonished, "We didn't pay them on time, making us responsible for the fees we caused." By this time, I was beyond pissed. Why was I having a conversation with full-grown men about taking responsibility for their errors?

How had this become a blame-the-victim situation? Did I mention, this was my FIRST day with the company? I was seriously reconsidering if I had made the right choice; they were probably thinking the same thing. As I looked around the table, most people were looking at their food or checking their phones. Those people knew I was right but had no intention of having my back. So, I proceeded to explain what is obvious to every kindergartener on the planet: if you make a mistake, you must accept the consequences.

Making excuses and blaming the victim is intentional Dick behavior. You are the problem, not in the Accidental to Intentional kind of way, but a full-fledged, Intentional Dick move. I spent the rest of lunch helping them understand why their justifications were ridiculous and ultimately moot. The Fair Labor Standards Act (FLSA)[9] requires employers to pay employees on the date established by their handbook, period. Yet, I felt obligated to respond to every inane rebuttal they had. I heard, "It's not our fault they don't have enough money in their account" and "No one should have bills set to autopay on payday", "If they can't handle their own expenses, are they reliable enough to work for us?" Someone even said, "We aren't doing our employees any favors by coddling their lack of planning." WHAT?! To be clear, a pay date is a contract between the company and the employees. If the company

9. FLSA is a federal labor law in the United States that is designed to protect the rights of workers by establishing certain basic labor standards for employers.

fails to meet its contractual obligations, they are required to cover all expenses related to the failure. More importantly, if you make over 6 figures a year, you do NOT get to judge the decisions of your employees making $12/hr. Believing that you can is an obscene demonstration of privilege and should be embarrassing. In short, you are the Dick!

Accidental

Not all "I am the Dick" situations are intentional. Like any other behavior, it can be accidental and as we've discussed in previous chapters, Accidental is the crossroads between Intentional and Conscientious. Recently, a company I work with experienced a similar situation, also related to pay. On the Saturday after the most recent payroll, the HR team received a frantic email from one of their employees stating that they had not received their paycheck. The email went on to acknowledge nothing could be done until Monday but expressed their frustration regarding the financial strain the missing paycheck caused. On Sunday, the HR director responded appropriately. She explained that the paycheck had been processed according to the payroll software records, so if it wasn't deposited into her bank account, it was most likely a banking issue, not a system issue. However, the director was also understanding and cc'd the finance department in case the deposit had been rejected by the employee's bank and requested the finance team follow up first thing Monday morning.

The employee did not agree with the director's assessment of the situation and replied, "I have been with my credit union for 25 years and they have never rejected a deposit." First thing Monday morning the finance team jumped in and started investigating the situation and by first thing, I mean by 7 am. Finance starts early to ensure all payment instructions can be processed in accordance with the international and domestic deadlines, at least that's what I've been told when I ask why all finance people start their day at the ass crack of dawn?

Upon review, it seemed clear it was a personal bank account issue. The payroll system confirmed the check had been processed; the company had not received a notice of a failed or rejected deposit; essentially, whatever happened was not a company issue, but a personal one. The CFO reached out to explain what had been discovered and offered to provide a live check to the employee and sort out the issue and possible overpayment at that time. The employee replied they would like a check and the CFO confirmed it would be available to pick up within 30 minutes. The situation wasn't an organizational one, but they prioritized helping the employee, even if that meant a potential overpayment, rather than defending their "rightness". They were practicing kindness, thinking of the employee's needs first and figuring out the issue later.

The employee was able to pick up the check by 8:30 am, unfortunately, the last name was misspelled on the check. The employee immediately notified them of the error. The CFO apologized for the mistake and explained the bank would most likely accept the check because misspellings happen, but he offered to print a corrected check. As the emails continued, the employee's anger grew. They expressed their frustration and irritation with the system and confirmed the bank had NOT rejected a direct deposit as well as reiterated the financial bind our error had put them in. This employee was venting all the frustration of the situation onto the company and tipped over into Intentional Dick behavior. Did I mention payday had been the previous Thursday, so there had been ample time before the weekend for the employee to notify the team? While the situation was stressful and unfortunate for the employee, they had some responsibility in the situation. Rather than working with the company, the employee was unfairly taking their frustration out on those trying to assist. As you might imagine, this was frustrating to the team as well and it was getting more and more difficult to be kind. It was clear the issue was not on the side of the company, but they were being Conscientious.

Conscientious

Meanwhile, with no sign that the original deposit had been rejected, the payroll team, before reissuing the corrected manual check, requested that the employee double-check with the bank regarding the missing deposit. Later that day, the employee sent a sincere apology, revealing that the bank had processed the paycheck early, and they hadn't realized the money had been deposited before the expected pay date. Despite the embarrassment, the payroll team, to their credit, refrained from gloating. Instead, they sent a final email advising the employee to contact them on payday if the direct deposit doesn't appear, emphasizing the importance of addressing such issues before facing financial difficulties. This displayed Conscientiousness—sharp but not mean.

The employee, in their frustration and panic, unintentionally behaved disrespectfully and hurtfully, blaming the organization without considering the possibility of their mistake. Rather than conducting further research, they persisted in their stance. However, two positive outcomes emerged: firstly, the employee genuinely apologized, a crucial step in practicing kindness, and secondly, the payroll team, historically known for being dismissive and condescending, seized the opportunity to enhance their reputation by responding with kindness despite being wrongly blamed. Their decision to avoid anger, dismissiveness or defensiveness prevented the situation from escalating further and showed true Conscientiousness.

"I guess it takes one to know one and two can play that game"

~Siobhan Davis

Chapter 5
A Tale of Two Dicks

As I have mentioned, my mom used to say, "It takes two to have an argument," meaning regardless of which siblings were fighting, we shared responsibility for the argument. Disputes and disagreements are rarely the sole creation of one party; instead, they arise through mutual engagement. This saying highlights the interactive nature of conflicts, where both participants play a role in the unfolding dynamics. Whether in the context of familial disagreements, workplace disputes or any other relational discord, if the conflict cannot be resolved it easily becomes what the Arbinger Institute refers to as collusion. Collusion is defined as, "A conflict where the parties are inviting the very things they're fighting against."[10]

Collusion occurs when a project, behavior or situation ceases to be productive and devolves into a battle for "rightness" which results in a mutually destructive collaboration where multiple parties, with competing interests and a lack of trust,

---

10. The Arbinger Institute. The Outward Mindset: How to Change Lives and Transform Organizations. Berrett-Koehler Publishers, 2016.

are unable to work effectively towards their goals. Ultimately, the situation becomes counterproductive and undermines the success of the project and the individuals involved. I call it an Intentional Dick Battle.

These battles rarely begin intentionally. Most of the time, it's good-natured coworkers and teams aiming to work together. Sure, there might be a few folks at work looking out for their own interests instead of those of the team, but often, it's just people doing their jobs, navigating life and trying to be decent in a crazy, fast-paced world.

If collaborators intend to work together as a team, how does it end in situations where logic has vanished and emotions reigns supreme? When we all agree to work together as a team for a bigger goal, how does it result in collusion; potentially leading to one or both parties departing for another department, company, or profession?

Competition for praise, personal insecurities and a distrustful culture set the stage for collusion, even with the best of intentions. Concerns about being judged or taken advantage of creep in and anxiety about the trustworthiness of colleagues starts to take over. However, collusion is not just about the colleagues involved but expands to the recruitment of others into their argument, catapulting the disagreement or conflict into a full battle. Still confused? Let me tell you a story.

I was working with a team in one of the larger organizations of my career. I usually prefer small to mid-sized organizations where I can oversee all aspects of HR, except for payroll – which I detest. But that's a story for another time. Unfortunately, just a few months after I joined, the HR department faced significant turmoil, resulting in the departure of both the department and division managers in quick succession, leaving a significant leadership vacuum and creating an opportunity for career advancement.

As is common in many large organizations, there is an internal pathway for career advancement, whether formal or informal. This organization's track was informal. Historically, the manager position was backfilled from the HR business partner position with an HR administrator moving into the vacated business partner role. There were four business partners, but only two who felt it was their job to have. The other two highly qualified business partners may have considered applying, but quickly backed out when the situation devolved into a scene from *Mean Girls at Work*, the unmade sequel to *Mean Girls*. Wait, I'm getting ahead of myself.

Conscientious

The team immediately came together to discuss how to share management responsibilities, distribute the necessary tasks and showcase the seamless collaboration within the team when unexpected challenges arose. The top priority was the success of the department, not individual achievements. There were open discussions about the level of interest each person had in the manager role, conversations about their varying skill sets and how that would play out in each scenario.

There are surprisingly few career opportunities where you have the whole stage to prove your ability to succeed, whether individually or as a team. The team made a commitment to maintain open communication and equally share all management responsibilities, including decision-making. A unified front was reiterated over and over, knowing that their collective performance was critical to everyone's success. Everyone was committed to collaboration, transparency, kindness and professionalism.

Accidental

However, this wasn't a Lifetime holiday movie, but real life with real people and no script. The first chink in the armor was the discovery that the position had been opened to external candidates. The minimum requirement for backfilling a position is an internal posting. It gives all employees the opportunity to apply while sending a message that the company has full confidence it can find an internal candidate. If an internal candidate can't be identified, then the position is posted externally. The job was immediately posted both internally and externally; sending the message that the leadership wasn't confident they would find an acceptable internal candidate.

Whether consciously or unconsciously, that decision undermined the cohesion of the team. If the leadership team didn't already see the hard work and skill set of the current employees, that meant none of the candidates had made an indelible impression. It isn't easy for someone to highlight their leadership skills while still collaborating fully as a team. As each of the business partners made the decision as to whether they were interested in the position, two final contenders emerged. The new kid on the block and the seasoned and senior team member. Both openly expressed their interest in the role, while maintaining a respectful and supportive relationship; still committed to continuing the collaborative approach and closing ranks to prove there wasn't a need for an external candidate. They continued sharing information and responsibilities while maintaining a friendly competition and a "may the most qualified woman win" attitude.

They were still competitors though and each believed they were the right person for the job. They started monitoring each other's behavior a little more closely, taking note of subtle changes and questioning interactions that were innocuous. For instance, the mail was being delivered to the senior team member directly instead of the department inbox. The new kid was scheduling one-on-one meetings with the division manager.

As they continued to watch each other, they became less and less trusting, attributing more and more malice to any perceived slight. *Was the new kid overzealous in building internal relationships? Was she disagreeing more in meetings and why was she meeting with the manager so often? What is she saying about me?*

Was the senior candidate having the mail delivered directly to her desk so she could cherry-pick the best projects and leave the less desirable and less visible projects for me? Was she withholding important information in hopes of becoming interim manager; hoping that if she was already doing most of the work, upper management would default the position to her without even conducting interviews?

Intentional

The air between them got colder as the tension in the office heated up and in walked collusion. Both started gathering allies on their respective sides. They looked for supporters in the team and throughout the organization; quickly pointing out places where they were cooperating and the other person was "cheating". This went round and round, the office atmosphere becoming increasingly toxic. It had become New Kid vs. Seasoned Employee. Rather than focusing on team relationships, they became more concerned with building individual alliances within the department and across the organization, especially with those who had close ties to the division manager. They were creating team division versus team collaboration. There was also a third team called #stayawayfromthecattybullshit, those people simply attempted to distance themselves from the drama and the battle that was brewing on the horizon.

The departure of the HR manager initially signaled a need for urgency in filling a key leadership role within the organization. However, the situation took a more critical turn when the division manager made an abrupt exit, elevating the need for a replacement to an immediate priority. While plans were already underway to expedite the hiring process through fast-tracked interviews and promotions, the unexpected departure intensified the sense of urgency.

In response to this heightened urgency, the organization recognized the imperative of appointing an interim manager swiftly. This interim leader would play a crucial role in overseeing our department, ensuring operational continuity and stability during the transitional period until a new division manager could be identified and brought on board. The absence of both the HR manager and the division manager underscored the significance of prompt and decisive action to maintain the organization's functionality and leadership structure during this challenging period of leadership vacuum.

What the team had not anticipated was that the interim role would be assigned to a manager from another department. When the news was announced, the two colleagues gathered their newly formed teams together to formulate a new plan. More accurately, they reaffirmed the original plan of working together without the need for direct outside involvement.

Moving back to the same team, circling the wagons against this unknown, potentially unwanted, usurper. However, this cooperation didn't last long. As soon as the candidates for the division manager role were announced, they split back into warring factions. Instead of learning from past mistakes and collaborating like true leaders, they found themselves divided once again. Neither one had truly moved back to Conscientiousness. Neither had committed to being kinder, more transparent, or less like a Dick; we were just being nice. So once the shock of the unexpected pivot had worn off, everyone chose a candidate to support, and the collusion was back in full swing.

The atmosphere in the HR Department had become almost intolerable. Seasoned Employee and New Kid were barely speaking, choosing to communicate via email, despite being 3 cubicles away from one other. As the hiring process drew to its climax, it became clear who had "backed the right" candidate, at least that's what the teams believed. However, when it was announced that everyone had to reapply and reinterview to be considered, the energy around the collusion evaporated. The process had gone on for too long and it no longer felt like anyone had an advantage over anyone else. So, they started mending fences, realizing one of them would be the boss and if the other wanted to keep their job, they would need to rebuild the relationship.

As the scheduled interviews approached, the candidates exchanged well-wishes and expressions of luck. In a display of camaraderie, they congratulated each other on the collaborative efforts over the preceding months and pledged to support one another, regardless of who secured the position. The interviews unfolded positively for both candidates, with each believing they had showcased their best abilities.

The Seasoned Employee, known for her organizational prowess and expertise in documentation, emerged as the go-to trainer for new hires. With an impressive efficiency that allowed her to match new colleagues at a rate of 4 to 1, coupled with three years of seniority, she brought a wealth of experience to the table. On the flip side, the New Kid, while lacking some technical skills, offered a fresh perspective on systems that required updating. Her strengths lay in building relationships, fostering collaboration, and working seamlessly as a team, providing a distinct and valuable skill set to complement the Seasoned Employee's qualifications. The competition between the two candidates showcased a balance of seasoned expertise and innovative perspectives, making the decision-making process challenging yet promising.

As they awaited the final decision, it became evident that both candidates had arrived at a mutual understanding. Despite the competitive nature of the interviews, they seamlessly transitioned back to working collaboratively.

The team quickly settled into a routine of cooperation, emphasizing their shared commitment to the collective success of the department.

Approximately two weeks later, the much-anticipated announcement was made. "Please welcome to the team... the new individual who previously worked alongside the recently appointed director in their prior position."

They had been right in the beginning; because they weren't able to get along, collusion had cost them both the opportunity. It was also clear that neither was prepared to be a good teammate, let alone the department leader. If either of them had stepped back from the battle, and behaved like the intelligent, kind people they were, things would have ended differently.

"You can still have a sense of humor and let someone know when they've gone too far."

~Rachel Simmons

Chapter 6
No Joke Zone

I personally believe laughter is the best medicine. In fact, in my family, the more uncomfortable, emotional, or stressed out we get – the more jokes we make and the less appropriate they are. Depending on the circumstances, we may be joking to ease the pain of a situation. Like the time I looked at my oldest brother, Martin, from the other side of our dad's hospice bed, waiting for his last breath and said, "This Sucks." All of us in the room chuckled and my dad took his last breath. He left hearing us laugh together, I believe he left on our humor instead of our tears. We also use the sharp end of humor to hurt, under the guise of a joke. Like the time I said to my brother, Sean, "You're a really good dad" after watching him with one of his daughters, and he quipped back, "Considering your taste in men, that's not much of a compliment." LOL. He wasn't wrong, my early 20s were a bit rough, but it also wasn't funny.

I believe humor and laughter are essential to coping with life's challenges, including in the workplace. Humor can play a significant role in developing rapport, reducing stress, and enhancing productivity. A study by the University of Western Ontario found that employees who have positive social interactions at work, including humor, are more productive and have better job performance.[11] Another study found that employees perceived humor to be an effective tool for building trust and reducing conflict.[12]

However, not everything is funny, and humor can be weaponized to dismiss or disguise discrimination and harassment in the workplace. Despite federal and state laws going back to the 1964 Civil Rights Act, sexism, racism, homophobia, and other forms of discrimination, are still far too common at work and in the world, see #metoo. In 2018, the U.S. Equal Employment Opportunity Commission (EEOC) found approximately 1 in 3 women and 1 in 4 men have experienced some form of sexual harassment in the workplace.[13] In 2020, an article in the Harvard Business Review reported, "Today some 40% of women (and 16%

---

11. Zhang, Zhen, Yam, Kai Chi, and Lehmann-Willenbrock, Nale. "The Role of Positive Social Interactions at Work and Job Demands-Resources on Affective Strain." Journal of Applied Psychology, vol. 100, no. 5, 2015, pp. 1311-1327.

12. Provenzano, D. A., Latham, G. P., & Steele-Johnson, D. (2016). Humor as a communication strategy in the workplace: An examination of employee perceptions. Journal of Business and Psychology, 31(3), 479-491.

13. U.S. Equal Employment Opportunity Commission. "Select Task Force on the Study of Harassment in the Workplace." June 2016, https://www.eeoc.gov/select-task-force-study-harassment-workplace.

of men) say they've been sexually harassed at work".[14] Yes, women can harass and discriminate, and men can be harassed and discriminated against. People of color can harass and discriminate against other people of color. Just like being a Dick is universal, harassment and discrimination can happen to, and be perpetuated by, everyone.

I am part of the 40% who have experienced sexual harassment and discrimination in the workplace. I am also the person who provides harassment prevention training and listens to employees who need to express their frustrations with a coworker or situation. Trust me when I say, it is happening in your organization at some level both intentionally and accidentally. Unfortunately, when the subject arises, the most common response I receive, whether by the accused or the accuser revolves around humor, "I was just kidding" or "I meant it as a joke" or "I'm sure they were joking" or "I shouldn't be so sensitive".

I did not report any of my experiences, and there have been considerably more than one. At least I didn't make a formal complaint. The reality is, I always told someone, but jokingly. I used it like armor to prove I was one of the boys and could handle the boardroom, secretly hoping one of them would tell me it wasn't funny, and that I didn't have to put up with it to be an executive.

14. Dobbin, Frank, and Alexandra Kalev. "Why Sexual Harassment Programs Backfire." Harvard Business Review, vol. 98, no. 3, May-June 2020, pp. 96-105.

I did a much better job at investigating reports I received from others than defending myself. I was wrong not to address the interaction in one way or another, but I was afraid. I was afraid I would lose my job; afraid no one would believe me; afraid I was overreacting; afraid I'd be ostracized; afraid of retaliation, etc. I am not alone, the EEOC estimates that "75% of workplace harassment incidents go unreported."[15] Unpacking the why is for another book, but the short answer is the victim risks more than the perpetrator.

Not all harassment/discrimination situations are equal. There is a range of harassment and discrimination, and egregious offenses are often the minority. In fact, I believe many circumstances can be addressed and dealt with by practicing kindness. The following stories are some of my most memorable challenges and resolutions.

I am not typical; if you haven't noticed that by now then I don't think you are really reading, but only skimming through the chapters looking for the "nuggets". Anyway, one of my colleagues was a wonderful woman who cared about and tried to take care of everyone in the building. She was also very traditional. We had many conversations about gender roles and assumptions, and she did not understand me at all. She

---

15. Equal Employment Opportunity Commission. Select Task Force on the Study of Harassment in the Workplace. "Report of the Co-Chairs of the Select Task Force on the Study of Harassment in the Workplace." June 2016, https://www.eeoc.gov/eeoc/task_force/harassment/report.cfm.

loved to make assignments based on her belief that girls were loving and creative and boys were rough and tumble and only good for moving things. I love her, but boy did we frustrate one another. The president of the company once came to me and said, "We didn't have any problems when you got here, are you trying to cause issues by bringing up issues that no one cares about?" To which I replied, "No, I'm protecting the company, like you hired me to do. Your assistant informed the party committee that the women were to show up one hour early to wrap gifts. Men didn't have to come because boys can't wrap gifts. That is blatant discrimination, like the definition and it's coming from a person who reports directly to you. Not good visuals dude." Okay, I might not have said the last part, but I was thinking it.

Her gender ideas were so ingrained, she didn't even notice when she made sexist statements or assigned projects based on gender. Bless her heart, no matter how many times I explained that I don't do "girly things" she insisted on enlisting my assistance when she couldn't be at a meeting. Like so many others, she didn't think she could be sexist because she was a woman and only men are sexist (this is false). Her unwillingness to hear or understand her misogynistic ideologies made her an Intentional Dick; a nice one, but she intentionally disregarded gender discrimination and my discomfort with her delineation of responsibilities. Additionally, her opinion of proper roles served as confirmation to the men in the building that they weren't sexist either, that's just how men and women differ.

One morning she popped into my office and said, "I'm not going to be here for the retirement party, can you grab the cake, plates, and napkins and carry them into the conference room?" I agreed to ensure the cake and the accouterments were in the room. That did not seem to be the same message the president received. When it was time to cut the cake, I brought it into the room, laid everything down and stood aside. In fact, I was headed back to my seat when I hear, "Aren't you going to cut the cake?" To which I responded, "You don't want me to cut the cake, I'm terrible at things like that." The room went silent; I looked around at the sea of men in the room and that's when I realized they were expecting me to cut and serve the cake and the thought that someone else could do it hadn't even crossed their minds. The owner was in the room, so it didn't feel like the right time to make a stand, so I turned around, walked back to the cake, and picked up the knife. I was pissed and I was embarrassed, and did I mention, I'm terrible at cutting cakes – I'm not kidding. I can't cut straight, I can't move the pieces smoothly from tray to plate, and I always end up covered in frosting. This event was no exception, as I tried to cut the cake straight and move the pieces onto the plates, I got frosting all over my fingers and several pieces had tipped over when I put them down. Additionally, the plates were just stacking up, no one was coming to get them, but waiting for me to deliver them. Every person in that room was being a Dick. My humiliation grew and I didn't know if I was going to make it through or break down. Luckily, the owner of the company realized my predicament and stepped in to help. He walked across the room, picked up two plates and handed them out. At seeing this, all the other male managers jumped up and started helping and we were able to get everyone a piece. I excused myself to wash my hands and sobbed for about 15 minutes in the bathroom.

I will always be grateful he stepped in to help because my humiliation would have been tenfold if I had broken down in front of everyone. He practiced kindness when he realized I needed assistance and jumped in to help, behaving like a leader in that room. They were all Dicks that day, whether they realized I was uncomfortable or were oblivious to the fact they were gender stereotyping by assuming that as a woman I would cut and serve the cake.

There was also another woman in the room, who remained silent for different reasons. Gender politics ran deep at that organization, and she was afraid for her own reputation and judgment if she was the one who had helped. The entire incident was based on discrimination and gender, but it was not a "reportable" offense. They didn't do anything illegal, they just assumed I would do it. They waited patiently to be served.

Not all the experiences were that innocuous. My first job after high school was in a small optical shop. It was a part-time job, close to my college and it was fun. I loved helping people pick out new glasses; I was learning how to measure the eyeline for the center based on the individual. There were only two employees, the manager and me. We got along well and often talked about his wife and kids. Then one day, when we were closing, he followed me into the back office. It was about the size of a hallway with a long counter that wrapped around the area. There was only one way in or out, but there was enough room for us to be comfortable if we were both working in the back.

I had my back to the door when I felt him behind me. He said he wanted to talk, but waited until after work hours because it was personal. My initial thought was to hope that everything was okay, but as I turned around, he was standing very close and blocking the way out. He talked about how beautiful I was and how he just knew we had a connection, I don't remember the conversation verbatim, but he asked me to have an affair with him. He had me pinned in the corner with no way out. The terror must have shown on my face because he backed up and let me pass. I ran out of the store and across the hall to the video store where my friend worked. I climbed under her counter and cried, I told her what happened, but she couldn't do anything. She even said, "It happens, you just have to get used to it." She did go over to the store to get my purse and keys, so I didn't have to, but the thing I'll never forget was what he said as I ran out of the store, "Don't try to report me for harassment, the last girl tried and guess who they believed."

The incident that bothers me the most, not for the experience, but because I didn't stand up for myself happened during a random drug test. If you've never experienced a random drug test day, you're missing out. I had been chasing down employees all day and I was exhausted. My last person for the day was the president. I had waited because it would be an easy way to end the day because he had given me the assignment and would be supportive and positive. Looking back, I'm not sure he believed he would be included in the random drawing, but that's how random works. Anyway, I was relieved to be almost done and ready to go home. I walked into his office, smiled and said, "Guess what? You are next on the list." He chuckled back, stood up and said, "Are you going to hold it for me?" I immediately responded with, "No" and my own awkward chuckle. He had once told me about leaving an inappropriate picture on a former secretary's desk as proof that some women can take a joke because she had laughed and laughed. She had thought it was HILARIOUS. The current situation, combined with the previous stories I had been told, made me certain he was being an intentional Dick. I was irritated, but not offended. I was certain he was just "joking" with me, purposely being risqué so I rolled my eyes, shook my head, and with as much humor as I could muster, which was very little, I said, "Let's go." That really should have been the end of the story, but the last shred of belief that this was just obliviousness and accidental disappeared when he decided to double down. It was clear I was tired and not in the mood for his "boys will be boys behavior", but instead of changing the subject he followed up with, "Do you ever do that for your husband?" Wait WHAT?! Had he just asked me that question? While I tried to untangle and process what had just happened, he followed with, "Sometimes my wife likes to hold it for me." To say I was speechless was an understatement. I literally had NO words, here was the president of the company, talking about his penis, and his wife and asking about my sex life, because he had to take a drug test. He thought he was being funny, but he was intentionally trying to make me uncomfortable. I was the HR manager, I should have shut him down, but do you know what I did . . . I said, in a sing-song voice as if I didn't have a care in the world, "Oh, you're so ridiculous," giggle giggle, "Can we go now?"

My response ended the uncomfortable topic and he bobbed along beside me happily chattering about something else. Meanwhile, I'm in my head trying to figure out what had just happened and what I was supposed to do about it.

First, I tried to brush it off. I told myself, "You know him; he doesn't mean it – he's just trying to be shocking and he thinks it's funny." A bit like Sean, knowing he was saying something controversial, but not with the intent to cause harm, just to be a Dick. Then I wondered if this was yet another test. I had been hired and technically reported to the corporate office and he'd been testing me to see whose side

I was on since I started. I wondered if he'd been purposely inappropriate to see if I would "snitch on him" to corporate? If so, that intentional Dick behavior was moving away from rude to dangerous. He had undermined my confidence both in my ability to do my job and whether my job was safe. Either way, I did nothing, and it has haunted me ever since.

I should have done something, not because he was being inappropriate, I truly don't get offended easily, but because it was my job to stand up and I didn't. I knew he had a propensity to behave this way and there were other women in the building that might be impacted by the situation. I didn't defend myself or the organization. I knew what I should do, but I was afraid; to lose my job, to be labeled a troublemaker, to be called a liar. Instead of doing the right thing, I decided to justify and ignore, thereby reinforcing the behavior as well as his power to do or say whatever he wanted without the risk of consequences. I told myself, he was just being a Dick, he's harmless and just thinks he's funny. I told myself he didn't intend to make me uncomfortable. At times, I even told myself that was the final; the testing was over and I had passed. Now I was part of the team. After all, he didn't mean it, he didn't hurt me, he has a lot of great qualities and cares about his employees and he's a good person. Later I did tell two other executives privately about what happened, they never reported it either. For the record, as a leader in an organization, if someone reports harassment or discrimination to you, you are legally obligated to report the information. They were also Dicks, for not standing up for me. For making me feel like I was making a big deal out of nothing. The least they could have done was to encourage him to apologize just in case he had made me feel uncomfortable. A heartfelt apology would have gone a long way. Instead, though I worked at that company for about 5 years and had amazing interactions with him, this is his legacy. This is the thing that I take with me, that I think of when I see him on LinkedIn or hear company updates. He's always going to be "that guy."

Laughter and humor are important tools for building relationships, communities, and strong organizations, but not everything is funny and when humor becomes an excuse for bad behavior it becomes a weapon of mass destruction; with the strength to take down an entire organization. Do not expect the secrets to last. More and more women and men are coming forward and telling their stories, reporting their experiences, or sharing them on social media. If you have been a victim of harassment or discrimination in the workplace, please contact your HR department. If you don't get assistance, call the EEOC or Department of Labor in your State. If someone reports an incident to you, take them at their word and report it yourself.

"Be kind whenever possible. It is always possible."

— Dalai Lama

Chapter 7
Kindly Accommodate

In 1990 the federal government passed the ADA (Americans with Disabilities Act) prohibiting discrimination against people with disabilities in public life; including in the workplace. In 2008, the ADA Amendments Act[16] (ADAAA) was passed which expanded the definition of "disability" and provided more comprehensive protections for individuals with disabilities. The law was intended to make it easier for individuals with disabilities to establish that they have a disability under the ADA and to obtain reasonable accommodations in the workplace. It also created the most ridiculous acronym ever. There are so many A's at the end, I'm never quite sure when to stop. The Society for Human Resource Management (SHRM) defines accommodations as changes or adjustments made to a job, the work environment, or the way work is usually done that enables a qualified individual with a disability to apply for

---

16. Americans with Disabilities Act Amendments Act of 2008. Pub. L. 110-325, 122 Stat. 3553. 26 Sep. 2008.

a job, perform the essential functions of the job, and enjoy equal employment opportunities.[17] Side note: this should not have needed to be written into law, but . . . Dicks.

In the workplace, implementing effective accommodations requires a thoughtful approach that balances the legal and ethical considerations involved with meeting the diverse needs of stakeholders. It can be cumbersome and overwhelming, requiring documentation from medical providers, negotiations and ongoing tracking. It can become frustrating and discouraging, making the manager irritated, HR exasperated, and the employees feel the opposite of supported. It should be an opportunity for expressing creativity, empowering managers to make front-line decisions and affirming to employees they matter. When that happens, and it does, it's a rewarding experience for everyone. Also, less paperwork.

When practicing kindness, the purpose behind an accommodation is to help and support your coworkers, friends, or even strangers. It is not just about disabilities, it's about life being unpredictable and hard. We're all in it together and everyone will experience a time when we need accommodation of some sort, whether continuous or situational. It doesn't have to be complicated.

---

17. Society for Human Resource Management. "Accommodation." SHRM Glossary, 2021, https://www.shrm.org/hr-today/glossary/pages/a. aspx#anchor-a.

In this chapter, we'll explore the various accommodations, some required by "law" and some envisioning company policy to be conscientious.

Susan was happy with her job. She loved the company she worked for and knew she was making a difference. Then she had a seizure, she had experienced 1-2 in her youth, but it hadn't happened in years. After a battery of tests, they didn't find anything and determined it was just a random event and there wasn't any evidence it would happen again. I didn't even realize that was possible, but according to the Mayo Clinic, seizures do not automatically equate to epilepsy or other long-term illnesses.[18] For obvious reasons, Susan was relieved and anxious to get back to work. Despite the good medical news, Utah law has a mandatory 3-month suspension of driving privileges for anyone who experiences a seizure.[19] Susan's job required driving, in fact, her job was to drive between clients' homes. It was a major function of that job. She wasn't going to be able to work for 12 weeks. She was covered under the FMLA, so she went on leave.

About 2 weeks before her driving suspension was lifted, she had another seizure. That second seizure changed the rules. Despite still not having a diagnosis, or an explanation for what was causing them, a 2nd seizure in less than 3 months

18. Mayo Clinic. (2021, April 30). Seizures. Mayo Clinic. https://www.mayoclinic.org/diseases-conditions/seizure/symptoms-causes/syc-20365711.

19. Utah Code Ann. § 53-3-220(3) (2021).

was going to require closer monitoring. It also meant her driving suspension would be extended for 6 more months. She was out of protected leave and allowing 6 more months of leave wasn't a reasonable accommodation, her clients needed a consistent provider. Susan realized immediately she wasn't going to be able to keep her job. In fact, she might never get to drive again. She was devastated, scared and in tears when she called to let me and her manager know. We were also heartbroken, we cared about Susan, we wanted to provide the support she needed. Instead, we were facing having to terminate a great employee due to a long-term medical condition, which would require continued treatment. This wouldn't only take away her salary, but also her health insurance; reason #216 the US needs universal health care, but I digress.

She still had a few weeks of protected leave, so we started to brainstorm, trying to figure out what on earth we could do to help. We offered a long-term disability plan, maybe she would qualify. Nope, she wasn't unable to work at all – she just couldn't do this job. Before the meeting, the director and I were discussing the situation and another manager walked in. Overhearing the situation – no HIPAA issues were being discussed – she piped up and said, "I'm about to have an opening in my department. She might be a good fit for that role." It wasn't exactly what Susan had done before, but she could stay with the organization she loved, and even see her previous clients when they came into the clinic. I was a bit apprehensive because she couldn't drive to the office and night staff positions were always onsite. Yet, the manager just thought for a moment and said, if she could get a ride to the office a few times a month, she could do the rest of her job remotely. And she does; she still has that position. We did not take away Susan's health issues, nor were we able to give her the job she wanted, but by practicing kindness we were able to keep Susan and provide some level of support and stability. It also confirmed to her that she was valued and needed, even with her changing abilities.

Medical accommodation is a matter of law, but not every situation requiring an accommodation is medically related, there are many opportunities to consider policy changes or small adjustments that can provide support to your employees and build a kinder culture utilizing empathy and common sense. Don't get me wrong, I'm in HR, I know policies and procedures, boundaries and guidelines are necessary. I write them and therefore I can say with absolute confidence that we cannot address every possible scenario. There is an expectation for managers, employees and leaders to critically assess a problem and make the best decision in the moment. For instance, the following accommodation was in direct violation of a standard company policy, and it was the right thing to do.

Jean was working for a large retail company with established policies applied across all their facilities. One of the policies was that non-employees were not allowed in the store when it wasn't open. This is a good policy for plenty of reasons, including the safety of the employees. But life happens and sometimes reasonable policies can change into unreasonable expectations rather quickly.

Jean had just been promoted to morning manager. This was her first managerial position and it included getting the store ready before opening for the day. One morning, an employee showed up and started the opening process, but they seemed a bit off. Jean watched them look out the window several times and then check the time. After about 10 minutes, Jean approached the employee and asked if they were okay. The employee quickly said, yes and immediately turned to continue working, but it was clear that it wasn't true. After a bit of prodding, the employee admitted they were anxious. They said, "my nieces are visiting, and we are going to spend the day hanging out when my shift is over, but they had to come with me, so they're outside in the car until we open. I left them the keys, so when it gets too cold, they can start the car to warm up again, I'm just trying to keep an eye on them." Did I mention Jean lives in Alaska?

She knew the non-employee policy was a strict one, it had been drilled into her during manager training, but she didn't care. She told the employee to go get her nieces and bring them in, the employee originally refused, not wanting to get Jean or herself in trouble as she was also aware of the policy and was not expecting an exception. However, Jean insisted and with obvious relief, the employee brought her nieces into the building and sat them next to the fireplace. They sat there quietly reading next to the fire until it was time to go. Jean violated a policy, probably one tagged with "immediate termination", because it was the conscientious and kind thing to do. Luckily, her manager also practiced kindness; when Jean explained the situation, the manager agreed with her decision. The risk of violating the policy was overridden by reality and kindness. It also was a one-time exception, with legitimate reasons for bending the policy. There wasn't an expectation by any of the employees that the policy was now null and void. In fact, they all appreciated the policy, it made them safer, and they knew it. All it did was send the message that the leadership in that store was thinking about them and would look for opportunities to help vs. quote policy and move on. Although they did opt to not share the incident with corporate.

Sometimes practicing kindness means bending a policy, but sometimes it means changing one. Tannisa works in an interactive studio where customers can observe and assist in creating a piece of art as well as purchase pieces made by the artists in residence. To preserve the safety of customers, the space was laid out precisely with a clear delineation between the studio and the forges. It was intentionally built to prevent injuries and keep the customers in the correct areas. She loves what she does and is honing her craft daily. She is also a single mom. During the school year, her schedule allowed her to drop off & pick up her daughter without issue. Then summer arrived and school let out. Now Tannisa had an 8-year-old with nowhere to go during the day. She had been scouring for options for months, all day care was too expensive and 8 was getting old to be in a childcare center. Camps and summer programs are even MORE expensive and only cover a short duration of time. Her ex didn't live in the area and couldn't take a shift and all her friends who could help, worked days too. She finally decided she would have to quit her job and get an evening job.

When she went to the owner, her boss, to resign they were surprised she hadn't said anything before, assuming she was unhappy in her role. Tannisa explained the situation and why she had felt she had to quit. She didn't want to leave, but she didn't know what else to do. This was a working studio and had dangerous equipment and delicate pieces of art; it had some very strict policies around safety and "touching things." The owner didn't want to lose her either, recognizing the importance of having the right person in the right role, at the right time.

Being a single parent, making barely above minimum wage and being unable to pay for daycare is not considered a disability under ADA. It didn't matter to the owners however, they just wanted to provide support to their valuable employee with a very tight budget that did not include a pay raise. So, they went out on a limb and offered to allow Tannisa to bring her daughter to work during the summer. They had to make some modifications to the space and to their safety protocols but that turned out to be an opportunity to discover better efficiencies with the changes. Not only was it a successful experiment, but they discovered ways to give her daughter opportunities to help in the shop. Which she still believes is the best job she'll ever have. Because Tannisa could be more present she started taking more responsibilities from the owners, which allowed them to take their own time off. Tannisa is now the manager and when necessary, her daughter comes into the shop and helps out. There is no longer a policy against bringing your child to work which does not equate to a free-for-all, with little kids running around a working studio, but it allows for discussion, for questions to be asked and alternative options to be considered.

We've talked about legal accommodations as well as reevaluating and changing policies for the betterment of the employees and the company. What if the request is so simple, it doesn't need a policy or law, but is just a request to have boundaries respected and kindness to be extended?

I love a good conference, but I hadn't attended one since COVID so when I found myself at a leadership conference alongside my Executive Team, I was slightly terrified. It was a function that boasted a relatively intimate attendance of around 100 individuals.

There had been assignments prior to attending the conference and I had been watching daily videos by a large and passionate doppelganger for Dwayne Johnson. He was getting everyone pumped up and ready to do real work when we arrived. There was homework and commitments expected of each attendee including following the 5 rules of the room: 1. Be Open; 2. Don't Hide; 3. Be Present; 4. All In; 5. Never Give Up[20].

As I stepped into the venue, a wave of apprehension and anxiety washed over me, not all of it related to the conference itself. The upbeat tunes emanating from the speakers set a lively tone, infusing the room with energy and anticipation. Facilitators and speakers strolled around, throwing out friendly hellos, engaging in conversations, and even sharing hugs while getting to know everyone.

As I navigated through the overwhelming sea of people, a sense of dread gripped me, and I made a determined beeline to the restroom. As I faced my reflection in the mirror, I gave myself a pep talk. "You are here to listen," I said softly, remembering the "Why" that had propelled me forward despite the spikes of fear that begged me to back out. Here I was and my mantra was, "I am here to listen and learn, not to talk," You know, a girl's gotta have some impossible goals.

---

20. Gali, Setema, Proceedings of Gamechanger, 2023

Cue Whitney Houston and Brandy in *Cinderella* belting out, "Impossible things are happening every day."[21] So, with that I walked out of the bathroom boldly and bravely into the darkened theater.

As I scanned the room looking for a place to sit, my attention was drawn to a front table occupied by four white men, prompting me to approach and request a seat. It's a peculiar quirk of mine to seek out the most challenging situations or individuals to convince myself of my own bravery. Instead of opting for a table with more available seats or one with women, I deliberately chose this table. Their conversation came to a sudden halt, and all four men turned towards me, resembling deer caught in headlights. Stammering responses of "Yes," "Of course," and "Please join us," they welcomed me to sit down. Pulling out the vacant chair next to a young man, we exchanged introductions. Suddenly, a burly man, white and bearing a resemblance to a leaner, slightly more muscular Chris Farley adorned with tattoos, approached the table. He warmly greeted one of the men, leading to an embrace and a brief chat. Subsequently, he went around the table, introducing himself to each person with hugs and cheerful exclamations of, "We're so glad you are here." As he approached me, he stood directly in front of my chair.

---

21. Rodgers, Richard, and. Oscar Hammerstein II, . "Impossible." Cinderella, directed by Robert Iscove, Produced by Walt Disney Television, BrownHouse Productions, Storyline Entertainment, 1997.

Normally, I am a hugger by nature, but I was already feeling frazzled and nervous; I did NOT want to hug anyone. I stayed seated, and I extended my hand. However, he insisted, stating, "This is a hugging place; we hug here," enveloping me and the chair in his massive arms as I leaned away, turning my shoulder.

The hug became more of a demand, and frustration and anger flickered in his eyes as he released me and stood back. Beneath the surface, there was also a mix of hurt and confusion, evident in his attempt to comprehend my reluctance. Engaging in conversation, the tension gradually eased. Unfortunately, as he prepared to leave, instead of respecting my preference for a handshake or a high five, he doubled down and said, "Now that we know each other, let's try the hug again." Swiftly objecting and stepping away, I found myself caught in a repeat of the initial uncomfortable embrace. As I looked around the table, I saw four other men awkwardly looking anywhere but at me.

Total Dicks – every single one of them – and completely intentional! My reluctance toward embracing the hugging ritual was crystal clear. The designated hugger approached me with what seemed like good intentions, merely trying to extend a welcoming gesture. Welcoming attendees and building enthusiasm for the event was, after all, his role. What started as an accidental misstep, however, turned intentionally dismissive of my discomfort.

This guy had numerous chances to be considerate, to acknowledge my evident unease and modify his approach. Instead, he adamantly adhered to his universal hugging policy, blatantly disregarding my verbal and physical objections, transitioning from unintentional to intentional Dick. I could see the displeasure in his eyes after each rejection.

To make matters worse, instead of letting the initial awkward moment pass, he intentionally went in for another hug, trapping me between him and the table once more. It was a situation that called for intervention, and the other men at the table should have stepped up. Let me be clear—I'm not someone who waits to be rescued by anyone, let alone a man, but they were there, witnessing the whole ordeal, and could have at least said something.

The first group activity was to find four people and give them welcome hugs. I thought I was going to die. Panic set in, and as I turned around, I spotted a woman making her way toward me. In a desperate, almost pleading tone, I put up my hand and muttered, "high five." She seemed taken aback but obliged with a high five. Curious, she questioned, "Don't you like to hug?" I responded, "Not strangers." Her sincere expression conveyed understanding as she remarked, "It's going to be a long week for you." She then pivoted to embrace someone else, leaving me to discreetly sit down, fervently hoping no one noticed my conspicuous absence from the hug exchange.

Around 30 minutes later, there was another one of those hugging exercises – this time, it involved ten people. However, I could have sworn I heard a mention of alternatives like a fist bump or high five. Everyone else seemed oblivious, happily embracing each other. Feeling overwhelmed, I dashed to the restroom and let out a few tears. The week ahead was shaping up to be a challenging one.

I'm not sure how the message reached him, but when the towering Polynesian man, who had been energetically motivating us through videos, learned there was discomfort surrounding hugs, he smoothly made an adjustment without explicitly addressing it. During the next hugging exercise, he subtly adjusted his language, proposing alternatives like fist bumps or high fives. It became evident that I wasn't the only one seeking relief from hugging, witnessing a growing number of attendees connecting without the need for physical embraces. This adjustment wasn't a legal obligation, but rather a gesture of kindness that made me feel heard and respected.

His actions showcased leadership that lived up to the values he promoted. It would have been easy to dismiss the situation as trivial, but he chose a path of accommodation and understanding. Instead of resentfully making the change and potentially shaming me through an announcement like, "Seems like some people here don't like to hug, so I guess we'll have to stop hugging just for the comfort of one person," he chose to be conscientious.

This story illuminates the choice we've been discussing when faced with being an accidental Dick, intentional or conscientious. Initially, "the hugger" embodied genuine warmth and innocence, but when met with resistance, his actions turned intentionally insensitive. Despite my evident discomfort, vocal objections, and physical efforts to avoid the hug, he persisted in his approach. Simultaneously, the other individuals at the table became intentional Dicks by standing back and doing nothing. Mahatma Gandhi said, "Silence becomes cowardice when occasion demands speaking out the whole truth and acting accordingly."

Contrastingly, the creator of the program demonstrated a conscientious choice when confronted with the unintended consequences of established interactions and learning styles. Adhering to his own principle of being open to feedback (rule #1), he chose to provide more than one way to build comradery. This proactive approach stands in stark contrast to the intentional insensitivity displayed by "the hugger" and the passive inaction of those at the table, showcasing the power of choosing kindness, adaptability, and leadership.

Guess what - that's not the end of the story. The very next day, the hugger approached me cautiously, stopping at a respectable distance, and sincerely apologized. The authenticity in his words, coupled with the genuine look of shame and regret in his eyes, granted me the power to let my guard down and afford him another chance. But wait, there's more; he turned out to be one of the speakers that day, sharing the entire story with the entire room, withholding the specifics of our interaction. Publicly acknowledging his mistake and offering an apology in front of everyone, including the men from the table, not only granted me peace but also created an atmosphere of mutual respect and understanding.

From then on, every encounter was punctuated with a smile and a high five, fostering an atmosphere of mutual respect, and understanding. Additionally, his act of kindness inspired others to choose differently. On the last day of the conference, I was in a breakout group with one of the men from the table that first day. At the end of the discussion, when it was "hugging time" he spoke up quickly and said, "Lindsay doesn't like hugs from strangers, so let's do a group hug."

At some point during the week, both men recognized the impact of their actions, or inaction and each made their own small adjustment. Yes, they had initially chosen a less considerate path, but they also proved that it's almost never too late to make a different choice.

Creating accommodations is not about making things complicated or burdensome; instead, the most impactful ones emerge from a foundation of kindness and respect. Whether it is something as simple as a high five, offering a warm and welcoming place to wait, implementing family-friendly policies such as allowing parents to bring their children to work, or even exploring alternative roles—accommodations are fundamentally about adopting a positive mindset and embodying authentic kindness.

A special gift is kindness
Such happiness it brings
When I am kind to others
My heart sings

- Sharon Steed

Chapter 8
Kindness Begins In Me

If this chapter seems like a repeat of Chapter 4, What if they Aren't being a Dick? You are half right. The concept is the same, but the intent is different. In chapter 4 we discussed being a Dick to others, this chapter is about being a Dick to yourself. Let's be clear, I'm not talking about thinking only of what's good for you or what makes you feel good at the expense of others. I'm talking about giving yourself breathing room for being human and that's a heavy subject that includes mental health issues and has the potential to be triggering. So, this chapter includes more direct quotes and resources from professionals.

There are two songs from my childhood that are the core of my life philosophy of practicing kindness. Both are from the LDS Children's Songbook, and they are seared on my heart and brain. "Kindness Begins with Me"[22] and "A

---

22. Ogden, Jillene. "Kindness Begins with Me." LDS Children's Songbook, Salt Lake City, UT, The Church of Jesus Christ of Latter-day Saints, 2005, p. 145.

Special Gift is Kindness"[23]. They may sound silly and trite. They aren't classics, they are just simple songs from church that make sense to me. When I heard them as a child, my young heart was moved. As I learned them, I believed them to the bottom of my soul. I still repeat them to myself daily, the lyrics to Kindness Begins with Me have faded leaving just the four words as a mantra.

Unfortunately, I forgot for a while, or maybe I never learned that kindness doesn't just begin with me, it belongs to me. It is a special gift I am allowed to give myself and a gift I am allowed to receive. I can't tell you when I forgot or whether I ever knew, but I can tell you when I realized how much of an intentional Dick I had become to myself.

It was my monthly meeting with an executive coach. I was sitting across from him in tears; exhausted and disheartened. I was tired of "ruining people's lives" and pretending it was okay because at least I was kind. I looked up from my drink and said, "I can't do it anymore, I can't fire another person."

He looked back and said, "So don't, let someone else do it."

I quipped back, "Who else could do it?"

He stayed calm, in his irritating way, and repeated my question back to me, "Who could do it?"

I realized his statement hadn't been flippant, but sincere and he was expecting a sincere response. I thought back to the

23. Steed, Sharon. "A Special Gift Is Kindness." Simply, 145A. Words and music by Sharon Steed, b. 1935. © 1969 IRI.

first time I had to fire someone. It wasn't great on so many levels, not the least of which was that I didn't have a clue what to say or do. I was the HR Manager and should have been the expert, but it was my first time.

The conference room was in the front of the building and directly across from the employees' workspace and that was our best option. There weren't a lot of closed spaces, I didn't even have an office. The manager and I had already determined what we would do. I would go in first and the manager would bring the employee into the conference room, they would sit down and I would say the words.

I walked into the cramped room with the scuffed table and mismatched chairs surrounding the table and pushed against the walls and realized I didn't know where to sit. I scanned the room while my brain quickly discarded each option I considered. I thought, if I sat at the head of the table, it would feel intimidating and awkward. So, I sit at the opposite end, it was closer to the door, but which seat? Should both the manager and I be on the far side, invite him to sit closest to the door or should he sit at the end with one of us on his right and one on his left. That didn't work, he would be swiveling his head back and forth while hearing his job was ending, right then. I opted to sit at the end of the table with the manager on the far side and the employee in the "escape" seat, the one nearest to the door.

Now you may be wondering why I was concerned with where to sit and how to be less intimidating, after all the result would be the same for him either way. This was not going to be a fun time, but I could not be a Dick. I didn't know the right way to do it, but I would do my best to be kind. Then I did what became my ritual before any termination. I put myself in his shoes and pictured how I would feel.

I don't remember exactly what was said, but I remember watching his eyes. Seeing the emotions flick through them, confusion, hurt, anger and then fill with tears. I remembered conversations we'd had about his life, being a single dad and going through a divorce, and negotiating custody and visitation time. I knew losing his job would further exacerbate his already stressful life.

After watching him drive away, I walked back into the building, past the front desk and the manager who wanted to debrief, I went through the lobby and straight down the back hall. I walked into the bullpen and made a hard right into Dylan's office. I shut the door behind me and burst into tears. My heart broke open and I just sobbed. I was riddled with guilt and self-loathing, how could I do that to another person, why was this my job? Dylan handed me a tissue and patiently waited for me to gather myself. When the sobbing slowed he said, "First time?" I snorted, half laugh/half sob, patted my eyes and nose with the tissue, and answered, between crying hiccups, "How did you know?" Followed directly with "I didn't cry during the meeting."

Without saying another word, Dylan opened his bottom desk drawer, this is a true story, reached in, and pulled out a bottle of whiskey and 2 glasses. He poured us each a splash (it was the middle of a workday), stood and handed me one and clinked our glasses together. He gave me a nod, shot the whiskey and sat back down. I looked back at him a bit stunned and then followed suit. He proceeded to give me a pep talk. He said my hurt showed how much I cared. He told me, he would rather be fired by someone who cares than someone who just marks it off their to-do list and moves on. His soothing and supportive words combined with the whiskey warming my insides calmed me and I was able to finish my day.

I appreciated his words and believed them. I also knew it was just the first one; it would not be the only one. I promised myself and the universe that I would approach every termination with kindness and respect, allowing the employee as much dignity as the situation allowed. I have kept my promise, not only personally, but by training others. I have been lovingly called the queen of terminations because I will volunteer to deliver the news, especially if I know the manager and I have different philosophies on the subject. So, why if this is a choice I make out of kindness, something that aligns with my core value, something I take pride in doing well, why was I ready to quit? Where was the happiness I was supposed to feel? My heart was not singing, it was screaming.

As I came back from the memory, I looked back down at my glass, smiling as I realized it was a whiskey in front of me, and it clicked. I over-examined every termination, looked for all the mistakes I made, and agonized over my failures. Rather than seeing the positive changes my philosophy and promise were making, instead of celebrating when it worked, I had internalized the worst parts. I worried about their self-esteem and their bills. I visualized them walking into their house and telling their family what happened. I imagined them blaming me, why wouldn't they? I was blaming myself. I held on to each one of these thoughts, letting them chip away at my sense of worth and drowning me with guilt.

For some reason, the parallel between the moments turned my kindness back on me and I saw the good I had done. I gave myself the same credit I afforded others. Specific moments of authenticity, comfort and smiles replaced the negative memories. I picked up the glass and finished the whiskey in a gulp, looked back at my coach, and said, "Me, and people I've been able to teach." Of course, this ah-ha moment didn't clear away the guilt, hurt and trauma that I gave myself, but it has allowed me to move away from being an intentional Dick to myself. Between therapy, meds and practicing kindness with myself, I'm in a much better place.

I am not the only one. It is not just me. I have seen employees, friends and family being unkind to themselves, taking responsibility where it wasn't theirs to keep. I'm not being dramatic or alarmist. These are real statistics. Life is not an easy experience, and if it is, you are doing it wrong. Things we face every day, things like trauma, illness, a pandemic or death are taking a toll on all of us. According to the National

Institute of Mental Health (NIMH), an estimated 51.5 million adults (20.6% of the population) in the United States experienced mental illness in 2019.[24] And in June 2020 a CDC survey revealed 31% of adults in the US reported symptoms of anxiety or depression and 26% reported trauma or stressor-related disorder symptoms related to the pandemic.[25] Whether you have a diagnosed mental health disorder, like me and my bipolar, or whether life is just coming at you fast and external forces are causing you anxiety and internalized guilt, it's happening to over half of the country, 57% according to the CDC. It is important to note that mental health statistics are complex and can be influenced by various factors, including systemic discrimination and cultural differences.

There is value in retrospect and guilt, it can be a positive function in that it can motivate people to make amends for their behavior or take corrective action to avoid repeating the behavior in the future. However, excessive, or chronic guilt can have negative consequences, such as anxiety, depression, or self-esteem issues. So, while guilt can have a positive effect, it is important to recognize and manage it appropriately. It's important to be kind to yourself and since I am still very

24. National Institute of Mental Health. "Mental Illness." NIMH, U.S. Department of Health and Human Serv ces, 2021, www.nimh.nih.gov/health/statistics/mental-illness.shtml.

25. " Centers for Disease Control and Prevention. "COVID-19 Pandemic and Mental Health." CDC, Centers for Disease Control and Prevention, 10 Sept. 2020, www.cdc.gov/coronavirus/2019-ncov/daily-life-coping/stress-coping/mental-health.html.

new to the concept of "kindness begins IN me", I went to professionals for guidance and inspiration. Let's jump in and let's see what we can learn.

Practice self-compassion:

Be kind to yourself and practice self-forgiveness. Speak to yourself in the same supportive and kind manner that you would speak to a friend.

> "Instead of mercilessly judging and criticizing yourself for various inadequacies or shortcomings, self-compassion means you are kind and understanding when confronted with personal failings – after all, who ever said you were supposed to be perfect?"[26]

My self-compassion practice is like my pre-termination routine, except I wear both pairs of shoes; giving myself the compassion I extend to others and then allowing myself to be the recipient of my kindness. For example, crying at work. I am pro-crying at work, as needed, not as a general rule. I work in HR, that's the hub of crying; except when working at a children's facility, then it's a toss-up between HR and the playground. Anyway, tissues abound in our office and tears are

---

26. Neff, Kristin. "Self-Compassion: An Alternative Conceptualization of a Healthy Attitude Toward Oneself." Self and Identity, vol. 2, no. 2, 2003, pp. 85-101.

welcome . . . except for mine. That is my natural feeling, crying is healthy, cleansing, and necessary, except for me.

Now, when I feel that way, I take a deep breath and say, "Lindsay, you get to have emotions. You are stronger with them. You are worthy." Then I, literally in my head, switch places with myself and repeat the words exchanging "you" for "I." "I am Lindsay and I get to have emotions. I am stronger with them. I am worthy." Then the two versions of myself in my head, hug. The point of that story, for our more structured readers (I do hope you're still here), is that there isn't a wrong way. Find something that you hear and believe and then practice. What do you think would work for you?

Challenge negative thoughts:

Question your negative thoughts and challenge them with positive and realistic ones. Negative thoughts don't tell the whole story. "The way to combat negative thoughts, and the feelings that go with them, is to challenge them with the truth."[27]

HR loves to ask probing questions and we love a good mystery. Whether it's interviewing or investigating, we are always looking for the full truth and I'm quite good at it. Yet negative thoughts in my mind are always given the benefit of the doubt. Let's flip the script. All negative thoughts are

27. Beck, J. S. (2011). Cognitive behavior therapy: Basics and beyond. Guilford Press.

required to bring evidence, argue against a positive perspective, and define how they provide value. Let's start right now. When I started my story about that first termination I said:

"It wasn't great on so many levels, not the least of which was that I didn't have a clue what to say or do.

Okay Lindsay, where is the evidence this is true? The conference room was visible, but not as visible as trying to use a back office. I did not design the building but made the best decision available based on the current architecture. I didn't know where to sit, but I took time to think about it and it worked quite well. I don't remember what we said, but I let him have a voice and before he got in the car, he gave me a hug. Let's try it again.

"It was a hard and emotional experience, but with some preplanning of language and logistics, he didn't know it was my first time."

That's better! "Challenging negative thoughts takes away their power and gives you back your power."[28]. Don't assume the negative is true.

---

28. Greenberger, Dennis, and Christine A. Padesky. Mind Over Mood: Change How You Feel by Changing the Way You Think. 2nd ed., The Guilford Press, 2015.

Create healthy boundaries:

Healthy boundaries involve understanding and communicating one's own needs and limitations while respecting the needs and limitations of others. It is necessary to say, "No".

"Every time you say yes to something you don't want to do, your body says no."[29] - Dr. Claudia Welch[30]

I have Hulk Hands. I don't mean the giant green toy Hulk hands you can buy at Target, although I think we have those too. I mean, my hands are really, really, strong. You know the scene in Harry Potter and the Prisoner of Azkaban when Harry gets so angry, he accidentally uses magic to break Aunt Marge's glass while she's holding it? While the Dursleys and Harry are freaking out, she just looks over and says, "I have a very firm grip".[31] That's me, I've done that, not the breaking a glass with magic, thing. That would be so awesome. Nope, I've just shattered a glass because I was holding it too tight. I also pulled the handle off my car door once, it wasn't locked and I wasn't angry, I just came off in my hand. Multiple IT

29. Welch, Claudia. "Every Time You Say Yes to Something You Don't Want to Do, Your Body Says No." HuffPost, 18 May 2016, www.huffpost.com/entry/every-time-you-say-yes-to_b_9932080.

30. Dr. Claudia Welch is an Ayurvedic practitioner and Doctor of Oriental Medicine who combines her extensive knowledge of Ayurveda, Chinese Medicine, and Western Medicine to treat patients. She is also an author and speaker, and has written several books on Ayurveda and women's health.

31. Harry Potter and the Prisoner of Azkaban. Directed by Alfonso Cuarón, Warner Bros., 2004. 00:53:28-00:53:33.

Directors have shaken their heads at me when I return my little laptop broken and ask for a hardier, heavier version.

What does this have to do with healthy boundaries, you ask? Well, it was one of the first boundaries I set for myself as I started down my healing path. I know I am not meant for delicate objects, craft projects, or small spaces so I try to avoid all of them. Unfortunately, people don't believe me or think I'm joking, at least new people. And because of my gender, I can only assume, I am always being asked to help with those types of things. Give me a table to move, it's much more my style, but that wasn't how it went. For years, I would feel sick every time someone asked me to help in the kitchen, set the table, or use glassware. When I have a choice between a glass or plastic cup, plastic every time. My discomfort was clear, and I inevitably dropped, spilled, or broke something, yet I still got picked for delicate duty and I would continue to say, "Of course".

I don't do that anymore. If I'm asked to do a task that requires dexterity and patience, I just shake my head and say, "No, let me know if you need a table moved, but you don't want me touching things you don't want to be broken." If that doesn't work, I make both hands fists, bang on the nearest hard surface, and say, "Hulk smash." That always works. The most important thing I do is stick to the "No" and refuse to feel ashamed. These are my capabilities, and I don't need to feel bad because they aren't feminine enough. What line are you ready to draw?

Seek and accept support:

Don't be afraid to reach out to friends, family, or a mental health professional for support and guidance. You don't have to go through difficult times alone. Seeking help is a sign of strength.

> "None of us got where we are solely by pulling ourselves up by our bootstraps. We got here because somebody – a parent, a teacher, an Ivy League crony, or a few nuns – bent down and helped us pick up our boots."[32] - Thurgood Marshall

I'm not being dramatic when I say, if I hadn't asked for help, both professionally and personally, I wouldn't be here writing this book. I don't just mean therapy and meds, although they are vital parts of my maintenance plan. I also reached out to friends and colleagues. I read books and listened to podcasts about leadership and mental health. I thought the hardest thing would be to ask for help. To admit I needed it. I was wrong. The most difficult thing I had to do was sit down, hold still, listen, and allow myself to be helped. It's a crazy thing I learned, no matter how much help you ask for – if you disregard the advice or support – it doesn't help. In my case, it further solidified my self-loathing. The truth was that I didn't know how to ask for or accept help, so I followed my

32. Marshall, Thurgood. "Speech at Holy Cross College." The New York Times, 19 June 1987, p. A17.

own advice, just don't be a Dick. As I mentioned earlier, I'm a certified trainer with the Arbinger Institute and it was during that class that I was reminded of the pathway in a train the trainer class for Arbinger Institute. Dave Moss was giving the class and he said, not verbatim, but this is what I heard.

As professionals you are accustomed to being the person with the answers, the subject matter experts, but now you are the students. You are not the subject matter experts. Do your homework and don't skip steps. And when you get stuck, look back to see what step you skipped.

"Do your homework and don't skip steps" is another of my mantras, and every time I start a new project, I tell myself at least 10x a day, "Do your homework and don't skip steps." When I'm frustrated and stuck, I ask myself, "What step have you skipped?" I'm not the only one, Denise reminds me not to skip steps, and Duffy reminds me not to skip steps. Pro tip: if you consistently hear the same thing from multiple people, you should probably take their advice. Otherwise, you're being an intentional Dick.

"Kindness in words creates confidence. Kindness in thinking creates profoundness. Kindness in giving creates love."

- Lao Tzu

Chapter 9
Leading With Kindness

Leadership is powerful. Leadership is the ability to guide, motivate, and influence a group of individuals toward a common goal or vision. Leadership goes beyond holding a position of authority; it encompasses the ability to inspire trust, foster collaboration, and empower others to reach their full potential. That's power, and power can be used for honorable or nefarious means.

Leaders are found in various contexts, including business, politics, community organizations and personal relationships; they are found at all levels of these places. Do not assume that because someone is in a power position, they qualify as a leader. True leadership requires more than just authority—it requires genuine care, empathy and compassion for others. It requires kindness.

Leadership rooted in kindness can create a lasting impact and foster positive change in individuals, teams and organizations. It goes beyond superficial gestures and embraces a deep understanding of the value of lifting others up. A kind leader recognizes that true strength lies in supporting and nurturing the growth of their team, building a culture of respect and inclusivity along the way.

Effective leadership requires both empathy and self-reflection. Empathy isn't just about understanding others; it's the art of stepping into their shoes, comprehending their thoughts and feelings. This skill, coupled with self-reflection, becomes particularly vital in navigating challenging conversations, difficult situations, and learning moments.

Leadership is synonymous with responsibility, and true leaders understand the weight of accountability that comes with their roles. Taking responsibility means owning both successes and failures, recognizing that the outcomes of a team or organization are ultimately tied to their decisions and actions. A leader who embodies responsibility fosters a culture of transparency, trust, and integrity. They don't shy away from challenges or pass the blame; instead, they confront issues head-on, learn from setbacks, and inspire their team by demonstrating resilience.

When leaders accept responsibility, they empower those around them to do the same, creating a collaborative and growth-oriented environment. Ultimately, taking responsibility is not just a duty; it's a hallmark of effective leadership that builds respect, instills confidence and lays the foundation for sustained success.

"Come on back, Sharon" I say as I push open the door, trying to give her a bright smile so she feels welcome, but most likely she is seeing in my eyes a similar look to her own. This is new ground for both of us. In 40 years of working, she'd never been fired and, in my 10 years of terminating people, I'd never agreed to meet with a former employee to discuss the termination. It's a rather big no-no. One of the reasons HR and Employment lawyers do not recommend it is because it can cause trouble. It can give the employee hope and potentially cause a case for wrongful termination. But here we were.

I invited her into the awkward corner space that was the HR office and invited her to sit in one of the uncomfortable chairs I had just pulled off the stack. Then I violated another firm HR rule and asked, "Do you need a hug?" She paused for a moment and then said, "Yes." As I put my arms around her, she started to cry and held on tight, "I knew I would cry if I hugged you, but I needed your hug." She stepped away and turned toward the desk and I moved the tissue box closer for easier accessibility. Sharon took a tissue as she sat down on one of the chairs in front of the desk. I took the other chair and turned it toward her. I took a deep breath, reached out and gently patted her knee, and said, "Sharon, talk to me". That was it, I said talk to me and then I listened. She shared her shock about the termination and her experiences up to and throughout the process.

As she talked, I felt slightly sick as I thought to myself, "What have I done?" I had clearly made a mistake, but it wasn't about the current meeting, the hug or holding her hand. The mistake had been not taking the time to talk to her before approving the termination. It wasn't illegal or unethical. Utah is an at-will employment state, meaning employers can fire employees for any reason or for no reason at all and at any time, as long as it's not discriminatory. No, it wasn't illegal, it was just a Dick move, and one I know isn't fair or wise. In fact, it was a rookie maneuver.

Once she had the opportunity to share her perspective, I took responsibility. I offered a sincere apology, extending regrets not only from myself but also on behalf of the decision-makers, acknowledging the mishandling of the situation. Directly addressing her, I asked, "How would you like to move forward?"

Sure, meeting up and offering apologies might not be the textbook approach, but they were the right things to do—conscientious and kind. And you know what? That's precisely why we managed to sort things out amicably, no Department of Labor (DoL) hotline call needed.

A crucial competency for leaders is the proficiency to communicate with impact. Leaders must articulate their future vision in an inspiring manner, motivating those around them. Additionally, they must adeptly communicate with team members, offering constructive feedback and guidance to foster a collaborative and supportive environment aware that effective communication goes beyond words; it's a mix of what's said, the context and shared understanding.

Non-verbal cues like body language, facial expressions and tone also play a big role in expressing intent. In non-verbal languages like American Sign Language (ASL), the definition of a sign is intricately tied to body movements and facial expressions; a shift in emphasis alters the meaning of a sign.

Verbal language faces the same challenge compounded by tone and volume. How you say something, where you look, and how you stand can completely shift the message. For instance, let's explore how body language and facial expressions influence the interpretation of the simple phrase, "I don't know."

Neutral:

- Responding with a shrug and relaxed posture signifies a casual, indifferent attitude, suggesting minimal concern for the question or answer.

Curious:

- Raising eyebrows and leaning slightly forward signals curiosity or intrigue, indicating a willingness to explore further.

Confused:

- A furrowed brow and slight head tilt convey uncertainty or confusion, reflecting a lack of clarity with the question.

Defensive:

- Crossed arms, pursed lips, and a sharp response signify frustration or defensiveness, portraying resistance or irritation.

Considering the various interpretations and potential for misunderstandings embedded in the seemingly simple phrase "I don't know" allows us to grasp the heightened challenges and potential for confusion when dealing with more intricate questions and responses. Now, the question arises: as leaders, how can you incorporate and apply this skill in your daily life? Start by assuming innocence and actively listening for understanding.

I first encountered the principles of effective communication years ago during a change management training session. This foundational idea has remained a fundamental approach ever since. The concept of assuming innocence as the initial step in fostering effective communication, often referred to as giving someone the benefit of the doubt, is paramount. The objective is to avoid hastily concluding that someone is being an intentional Dick. Instead, try to understand the simplest explanation and then ask follow-up questions for additional clarity.

In your pursuit of clarity, it's crucial to be ready to actively listen for understanding, extending beyond the surface of mere word-hearing. This involves acknowledging the multifaceted aspects of communication we explored earlier, encompassing tone, volume, body language and facial expressions. Stephen Covey states, "most people do not listen with the intent to understand; they listen with the intent to reply." Leaders not only listen to understand, they also understand listening is multifaceted and the words are only part of the communication.

Early in my career I was given the opportunity to lead a process change project. We had been experiencing miscommunications between the membership and finance departments. As I researched the issue, I discovered it was truly just a miscommunication that was easily solvable. I reached out to my counterpart, Taylor, in the accounting department to schedule a meeting She was less than receptive, but reluctantly agreed. I had sent my proposal to the managers in both departments prior to our meeting for approval, and everyone seemed to be on board. I was excited and nervous the day of the meeting because it was my first time running a meeting. I arrived in the conference room first. I had printed copies of the proposal for each attendee; I set out snacks and water and I anxiously awaited everyone's arrival.

The last person to arrive was Taylor from accounting. The moment she walked into the room it was clear she did not want to be there. Her back was rigid, she had a scowl on her face, and wouldn't make eye contact with anyone in the room. She sat down with a sigh and loudly dropped her notebook on the table. She hadn't said anything, but her body language and energy were a clear message. That did not help my nerves. As I started the discussion her eyes darted up and straight into mine. They were fiery and my voice cracked a little, but I gathered myself together and started walking everyone through the proposal. Again, Taylor didn't say anything. She flipped through the proposal quickly and then turned it over with a harrumph, sat back in her chair and crossed her arms.

I tried to ignore her as I started again, but I could feel her cold stare as I tried to make my presentation. Part of me wanted to cry and crawl under the table; part of me wanted to scowl back at her, maybe even stick out my tongue at her and say something witty, but hurtful. There was another part too. I had just recently attended change management training and the words, "assume innocence" ran through my head. So, I put my proposal down, crossed my hands over the paper and looked directly at her. Then I said, "Taylor, are you upset about something?" She was startled by my question and mumbled something like, "No, it's fine!" I didn't back down though. I just looked at her again and said, "I don't think we'll get very much done here if you're not onboard." She really didn't appreciate that and responded, "I don't like this whole thing, I don't appreciate you just showing up and telling me I'm doing my job wrong."

At that moment I understood her behavior, she was feeling threatened and defensive about the meeting. She believed I was trying to make her look bad and myself good. I gazed over at her and replied, "I'm not trying to tell you how to do your job, I'm asking you how I can do my job better and make sure I provide you with all the information you need. I'm looking for solutions to help you, not make things harder." She looked at me for a moment and then just said, "Oh, okay." That was it, her body visibly relaxed. Gone was the scowl and the harrumphs. She reopened the packet and we got down to work.

Conclusion

Congratulations, we've reached the finish line. When tackling the art of paper writing in college, professors often emphasize that an introduction sets the stage, the chapters deliver the content, and the conclusion ties it all together. So, let's do a quick rundown.

A Dick is defined by behavior, not necessarily a personality trait; although we know it can be - note my brother. It describes language, behavior or actions that cause harm to another human being. I use the term Dick because it works for me, but one of the ways to practice kindness is to leave space for other people's language and comfort level. It can be exchanged with jerk, asshole, or even knucklehead, as long as it sticks. The point is to make it easy to remember because it can be easy to do. Don't be a Dick is catchy and will sit in the back of your mind and fester.

There are 3 types of Dicks: Intentional, Accidental and Conscientious. Intentional Dicks may display a range of negative behaviors, such as belittling or mocking others, using offensive language, engaging in bullying or harassment, or purposefully causing emotional distress. They often use jokes and sarcasm to disguise their behavior, but their actions are driven by a lack of empathy and a disregard for the well-being and feelings of those around them. However, they can still practice kindness. In fact, you can be an Intentional Dick in one facet of your life or one type of situation and exceptionally kind in another.

Accidental Dicks inadvertently act in a rude, thoughtless or inconsiderate manner. They do not have malicious intentions or a deliberate desire to cause harm. Their actions may result from a lack of awareness, social clumsiness or simply a momentary lapse in judgment. They may occasionally exhibit rude or thoughtless behavior due to temporary circumstances, stress or lack of awareness.

They may also say or do something that comes across as insensitive, offensive, or hurtful without intending to do so. It could be a thoughtless comment, a poorly timed joke, or an action that inadvertently upsets or offends others. However, They can quickly be exposed as Intentional based on their reactions. They are typically open to feedback, willing to apologize and are genuinely remorseful once they become aware of the impact of their actions. It is important to approach them with understanding and empathy, as they often do not have ill intentions behind their behavior. Just like Accidental Dicks can become intentional, they can also become conscientious. Communicating openly and constructively with them can help raise their awareness, encourage them to be more mindful of their words and actions and foster a more considerate and respectful social environment.

The Conscientious Dick is trying. They emphasize their aspiration to be better and highlight their conscious efforts to be kind. They are committed to self-improvement and the desire to foster positive relationships with others. Depending on their relationship with the person they are talking to, they can have light-hearted, playful and friendly banter. It is typically characterized by humor, lighthearted sarcasm, or gentle ribbing. They use teasing not to hurt or demean the other person but to create a sense of camaraderie, build rapport or engage in playful interaction.

Kind can be nice, but being nice doesn't make you kind. Kindness goes beyond surface-level politeness and reflects a genuine concern for the well-being and happiness of others. It involves acts of compassion, empathy and understanding; it is driven by an innate desire to alleviate suffering or bring joy to others. Kindness often involves thoughtful actions, words, or gestures that are rooted in empathy and a genuine desire to make a positive difference in someone's life. It is a trait that is consistently practiced and extends beyond superficial niceties. Kindness is about being considerate, supportive, and respectful towards others, even when faced with challenges or differences.

Being nice typically refers to displaying pleasant or agreeable behavior toward others. It often involves politeness, courtesy, and socially appropriate behavior. While niceness can contribute to positive interactions, it could be driven by a desire to avoid conflict or maintain social harmony, rather than genuine concern for others' well-being. Niceness may not always reflect an authentic emotional connection or deeper empathy. It can sometimes be superficial or transactional, where the focus is on maintaining a positive image or receiving social approval.

Kindness is an inherent quality that stems from empathy and genuine care for people, while niceness can be more socially driven, focused on external appearances or avoidance of difficult conversations. Kindness emphasizes the importance of understanding and compassion, fostering positive connections and making a meaningful impact in the lives of others. You can be nice and kind, but just being nice doesn't mean you are being kind.

Kindness is not a sign of weakness. In fact, kindness is a strength that requires courage, empathy and compassion. It takes strength to put aside one's own needs or desires and genuinely care about the well-being of others. Wayne Dyer says, "If you have the choice between being right and being kind, choose kind", that can take superhuman strength. Kindness is not about being passive or allowing yourself to be taken advantage of, but rather it's about approaching conflicts and differences with understanding and empathy, seeking win-win solutions and promoting a more inclusive and cooperative organization. It does not mean disregarding our own boundaries or enabling harmful behavior. Kindness should be accompanied by assertiveness and a commitment to justice. It means standing up against injustice, advocating for the rights of marginalized group and challenging systems that perpetuate discrimination. True kindness requires us to be aware of power imbalances and actively work towards creating a more equitable and inclusive society.

There are times and situations where we believe we are right, but we're being the Dick. Practicing kindness requires us to overcome our own biases, ego and self-interests. When you put your ego aside to practice kindness, you let go of the need to be right, superior or in control; you become more aware of the impact your actions and words can have on others and you actively choose to act with empathy, compassion and understanding. This involves listening attentively to others, considering their perspectives and feelings, and treating them with respect and dignity. Putting your ego aside also means being humble and open-minded. It requires acknowledging that you don't have all the answers and being willing to learn from others. It involves being willing to admit when you're wrong, apologizing when necessary and making amends to rectify any harm caused.

One Dick can cause a toxic environment but when you have dueling Dicks your workplace can become intolerable; often causing good employees to leave to avoid choosing sides in the battle raging in the department or company. The Arbinger Institute calls it collusion and it includes each Intentional Dick recruiting others to their side by highlighting themselves positively, suggesting another person is deceitful or jealous and spreading dissent and distrust. When leaders are faced with these types of situations, whether as an observer or participant, it is up to them to stop being a Dick and bring the collusion to an end. This can happen in different ways, such as finding common ground. Seek areas of agreement and focus on shared objectives. Actively look for the benefits of working together toward a common purpose and highlight the collective impact that can be achieved.

Practicing kindness could also be establishing or reestablishing trust. Be honest, reliable, and consistent in your interactions. Demonstrate integrity and show that you value and respect the perspectives and contributions of others, even if you don't agree with them. Offer to provide support, resources, or expertise demonstrating your collaboration isn't one-sided.

While humor is a valuable tool, some things aren't funny. Harassment and bullying of any kind in the workplace are not funny. That includes unwelcome or offensive behavior, whether verbal or physical, that targets an individual based on protected characteristics such as sex, race, religion, disability, or sexual orientation. It creates a hostile and toxic environment that can cause emotional distress, harm, and hinder an individual's ability to work and thrive. Humor should never be used as an excuse or justification for harassment. Making jokes or engaging in behavior that is disrespectful, demeaning or discriminatory toward others is not acceptable and can have serious consequences. It perpetuates harmful power dynamics, undermines inclusivity and violates the rights and dignity of others.

Workplace culture should promote respect, equality and professionalism. Creating an environment where all employees feel safe, valued and free from harassment is crucial for their well-being and overall organizational success. It is essential to educate employees about the importance of maintaining respectful interactions and to have clear policies and procedures in place to address any instances of harassment promptly and effectively. Harassment in the workplace is a serious matter and should never be trivialized or treated as humorous because it's not funny. It is essential to promote a workplace culture that upholds respect, inclusivity and dignity for all employees.

Don't be a Dick to yourself. You are worthy of kindness and you need to receive it from yourself. Practice self-compassion and self-forgiveness. Talk to yourself in the same voice you would use on your friends. Challenge negative thoughts; refuse to automatically believe them. Negative thoughts need to prove their worth. Give your positive thoughts the benefit of the doubt instead. If you are going to believe something without proof, choose the positive. Don't berate yourself for mistakes, we all make them. Use them as learning opportunities, that's how practice works. Set realistic expectations and practice self-care. Take care of yourself physically, mentally and emotionally. Eat well, exercise and make time for activities that bring you joy and relaxation. But don't set impossible standards for yourself. Be realistic and set achievable goals.

Ask for and accept support. You are not alone. You deserve help when you need it and there are plenty of resources available. Connecting with trusted friends and family members can provide a strong support network. They can offer a listening ear, empathetic understanding, and practical assistance. Sharing your challenges and seeking their support can help alleviate stress and provide comfort.

Engage the services of a mental health professional, such as a therapist, counselor or psychologist. Ask your employer if they offer an Employee Assistance Program (EAP). Professionals are trained to provide guidance, offer coping strategies and help you navigate through challenging situations. They provide a safe and confidential space for you to express your thoughts and emotions without judgment.

Join a support group, either in-person or online, to connect with individuals who are going through similar experiences. Support groups create a sense of community, where you can share your struggles, learn from others and gain valuable insights and coping mechanisms.

Online resources such as websites and forums, provide valuable information, tools and support for various mental health concerns. You can access educational materials, self-help resources and even connect with mental health professionals through virtual platforms.

In times of crisis or immediate need, helplines and hotlines can provide immediate support and guidance. These services are often available 24/7 and offer a listening ear, crisis intervention and referral to appropriate resources. Remember, seeking support is a sign of kindness and that takes strength.

Kindness in leadership is a valuable and transformative quality that has numerous positive effects on individuals and organizations. Kind leaders foster positive and supportive relationships and treat others with respect, empathy and compassion, creating an environment of trust and psychological safety. This leads to stronger bonds, improved teamwork and increased employee satisfaction.

Kind leaders are effective communicators. They actively listen to their employees, value their perspectives and provide constructive feedback in a respectful manner. They prioritize the growth and development of their team members. When leaders choose not to be a Dick, they set the tone for a positive organizational culture. They model kindness and promote a culture of respect, inclusivity and support, which permeates throughout the organization.

Each act of kindness, no matter how small, has the power to make a profound difference. By implementing a philosophy of kindness at work and personally, you have the capacity to challenge the status quo, dismantle harmful systems and build a workplace and society rooted in kindness and justice. Remember, kindness is not a passive endeavor but an active and intentional choice we make every day. It requires courage, vulnerability and a willingness to step outside of our comfort zones. It requires conscientious decisions and reactions. *If you find it hard to be kind... just don't be a Dick!*

Meet The Author
Lindsay K. Mattes, MAOL

Lindsay Mattes is a Business Owner, seasoned Executive HR Strategist, International TedX Speaker, and Author, dedicated to fostering compassion and empathy in the workplace and the world. As President and Founder of KINDHR, she leverages her broad knowledge and experience to partner with leaders to impart and embody the transformative power of kindness, summarized in her leading principle: "Don't be a Dick".

Lindsay's professional journey underscores the significance of strategic planning, leadership development, and the cultivation of a culture of kindness within organizations. She firmly believes that by prioritizing kindness, businesses can establish inclusive environments that enhance employee well-being, fuel creativity, and drive collaboration, ultimately leading to success in today's competitive landscape.

Lindsay's expertise has led to invitations to speak at diverse conferences, and events, including the TedX stage. Lindsay was named a *2024 HR Achievement Award Honoree* by Utah Business and Utah SHRM for her contributions to changing the way Utah employees are hired, developed, nurtured, and retained. Amidst significant shifts in the workforce and the world at large, Lindsay acknowledges the collective responsibility we share in shaping the future. She is deeply passionate about this transformative era and is committed to enhancing organizational culture, fostering personal growth, and strengthening community bonds through kindness.

Lindsay's involvement extends beyond her professional endeavors, notably as a dedicated volunteer in various board positions. She has served as Programming Director for the Salt Lake chapter of SHRM (SLSHRM), the Certification Director for Utah SHRM, and co-chaired SLSHRM's inaugural Talent Acquisition conference. Lindsay currently serves as the Board President for Utah's Repertory Dance Theatre (RDT), the nation's pioneering modern dance repertory company committed to modern dance's creation, performance, perpetuation, and appreciation.

Lindsay holds both the SPHR and SHRM-SCP HR certifications. She has a bachelor's degree in Women's Studies from the University of Utah and a master's degree in Organizational Leadership from Gonzaga University, specializing in Servant Leadership.

Lindsay lives in Utah. She has been married for 22 years, has 4 daughters, 1 son-in-law, 3 dogs, 6 chickens, and 1 miniature rooster.

Website: www.lindsaymattes.com
Email: lindsay@lindsaymattes.com
LinkedIn: www.linkedin.com/in/lindsaykmattes

www.ingramcontent.com/pod-product-compliance
Lightning Source LLC
Chambersburg PA
CBHW051206120626
46547CB00013B/1221